Curiosities Series

MASSACHUSETTS
Curiosities

QUIRKY CHARACTERS,
ROADSIDE ODDITIES, & OTHER
OFFBEAT STUFF

Bruce Gellerman
and Erik Sherman

The Globe Pequot Press

GUILFORD, CONNECTICUT

The data listed in this guidebook was confirmed at press time. We recommend, however, that you call establishments to obtain current information before traveling.

Text design by Bill Brown
Layout by Deborah Nicolais
Maps by XNR Productions © The Globe Pequot Press

Front cover photos: Hilltop Steakhouse and Cohasset light by Erik Sherman, and the Weathervane restaurant and the Skinny House by Bruce Gellerman.
Back cover photo: Hood Milk Bottle by Bruce Gellerman.

ISSN 1550-6932
ISBN 0-7627-3070-6

Manufactured in the United States of America
First Edition/First Printing

For Yulia, Andre, and Anna,
who make life infinitely curious.
—B.G.

To my parents, who taught me to question
the wisdom of convention.
—E.S.

Help Us Keep This Guide Up to Date

Every effort has been made by the authors and editors to make this guide as accurate and useful as possible. However, many things can change after a guide is published—establishments close, phone numbers change, and facilities come under new management.

We would love to hear from you concerning your experiences with this guide and how you feel it could be improved and kept up to date. While we may not be able to respond to all comments and suggestions, we'll take them to heart and we'll also make certain to share them with the authors. Please send your comments and suggestions to the following address:

The Globe Pequot Press
Reader Response/Editorial Department
P.O. Box 480
Guilford, CT 06437

Or you may e-mail us at:
editorial@GlobePequot.com

Thanks for your input, and happy travels!

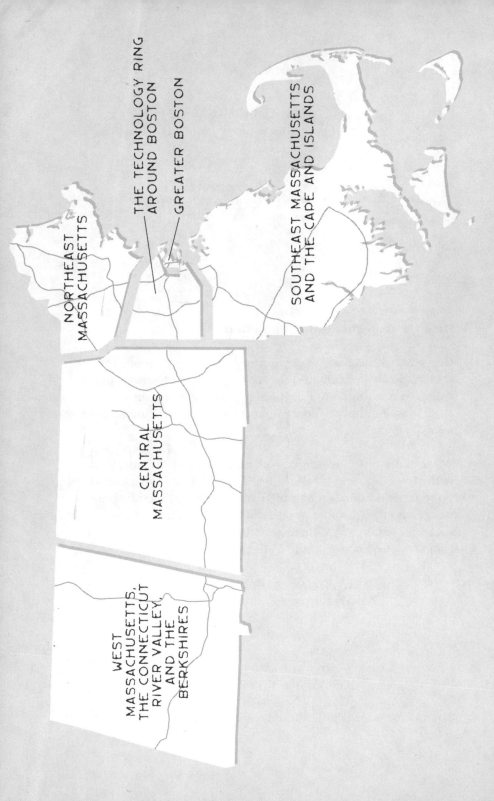

NORTHEAST MASSACHUSETTS

THE TECHNOLOGY RING AROUND BOSTON

GREATER BOSTON

SOUTHEAST MASSACHUSETTS AND THE CAPE AND ISLANDS

CENTRAL MASSACHUSETTS

WEST MASSACHUSETTS, THE CONNECTICUT RIVER VALLEY, AND THE BERKSHIRES

CONTENTS

ACKNOWLEDGMENTS

As powerful as the Internet is in collecting the flotsam and jetsam of life, curious people are still the best sources for Massachusetts minutiae and we are indebted to many for sharing their knowledge and digging deep when we set them to task.

To Deborah Douglas, curator of science and technology at the MIT Museum, many thanks for introducing us to Kismet, the world's most emotive robot. Craig Le Moult and Siobhan Houton of Tufts University helped show us which way was up regarding the antigravity monument and the tale and tail of Jumbo, the elephant. Prof. Gordon Prichett from Babson College can actually tell you what an apple from Newton's tree tastes like, and we were blessed to make the acquaintance of Diane Shephard, archivist at the Lynn Museum, who introduced us to the God Machine.

Thanks, too, to Stephan Nonack, head of Reader Services at the Boston Athenaeum, who gave us the lowdown on the "skin book," and to Jennifer Spencer for opening up her skinny house. Roberta Zonghi, the keeper of rare books and manuscripts at the Boston Public Library, was a font of information about things curious about Boston, as was the entire staff at the Boston Historical Society. And the Worcester Historical Society is second to none when it comes to being friendly and helpful.

Heidi Wellman at Chandler's General Store in Colrain helped by providing information on Old Glory and getting us the inside scoop on the Arthur B. Smith covered bridge. Kate Wellspring, collections manager at Amherst College's Pratt Museum, offered a firm footing on dinosaur tracks, as did Kornell Nash.

Jarvis Rockwell was unfailingly generous with his time as we asked about his toy collection, and the staff of the Country

Charm Restaurant in Cheshire didn't blink an eye while seriously answering the question, "Just how tall is that rooster statue on the top of your building?" And a Global Positioning System enthusiast, with the handle Khao Mun Gai when he indulges in the sport of geocaching, led us to the Forty-Second Parallel marker.

David Olson and Susan Abele at the Newton History Museum at the Jackson Homestead always took our requests for information with a straight face, whether we were inquiring about Fig Newtons or worm farms. Chet Kennedy, founder of the Public Health Museum, is a man with a mission and a missionary zeal; and Rev. Steven Ayers, vicar of the Old North Church, was always ready with a quip and a quote about colonial Boston.

Ellen Berlin of the Boston Medical Center set us straight on the fate of Jack the Duck. Charles Ball, the president of World Smile Day, was a delight to work with. And we'll always remember Tom Smith from Woburn City Hall for remembering the *Maine* cowl and telling us about it.

If you want to know about the smallest church in the world, the Hudson Public Library and Vic Petkauskos are the place to go. Bert Cohen knows more about marbles than any person in the universe, and if you are really into bad art, the person to see is Louise Sacco, curator of the Museum of Bad Art. Deborah Henson-Conant has a taste for burnt food and curates her crispy critters and tofu dogs with aplomb. Dr. Stephen Gould is one of those rare people who actually stops and reads roadside monuments. Thanks to him for pointing out where "Jingle Bells" was written.

And many thanks to Marc Abrahams, editor and founder of the *Annals of Improbable Research,* for thinking we were curious enough, or just crazy enough, to write this book. We hope we've proven you correct on both counts.

INTRODUCTION

After working on a book like this for a while, you no longer get embarrassed by asking such questions as, "Excuse me, do you know where Mary's little lamb is?" or "Are Jumbo the elephant's ashes kept in a jar of plain or crunchy peanut butter?" or "Where can I find the world's largest thermometer collection?" Yes, those around you still look at you cross-eyed, but you no longer mind: It just goes with the territory of being curious about Massachusetts, as curious a place as ever there was. After all, it got its start by Pilgrims who couldn't stand intolerance and European persecution, and who thus fled to a new land where they could have the freedom to persecute and be intolerant of everyone else. Upon reaching Cape Cod, one of the first acts of this largely religious group was to steal corn that Indians had stored for the winter. After finally coming to their last stop—which they still thought was somewhere in Virginia—the Pilgrims set up the first public utility, a grain mill. (You can thank them for hundreds of years of misbillings and poor customer service.) And you thought they survived that first winter on turkey? We're lucky we're not munching on a giant loaf of corn bread for Thanksgiving

You might think it easy to distill Massachusetts into a combination of Puritanism, rocky soil, and history—an image set in native granite: predictable, solid, inflexible. We thought the same when each of us moved here decades ago. And, like us, you are in for a surprise. Massachusetts is a contradictory land, full of unusual people, places, objects, ideas, and cranky misfits. Talk about ornery: The settlers couldn't even form a state, and instead chose to create a commonwealth.

Perhaps political unrest and opposing the usual order of things was a healthy release for the residents, because all you have to do is look at what happened when there wasn't some government to overthrow, action to protest, or election to contest. A colonial daredevil decided to challenge Puritanical Bostonians by flying from atop the Old North Church—more than 150 years before the Wright Brothers. The city leaders' reaction? You'd think that they'd be thrilled at the technical marvel. Nope. They got annoyed and banned flying. And what can you say of a place where people build giant seahorses and large granite towers, for the sole purpose of marketing? Or where a golf course includes an eighteenth-century grave or a monument to modern rocketry? Speaking of graves, you don't have to dig far to find some very curious final resting places. Massachusetts is the last stop for Jumbo, Mother Goose, and Mary Baker Eddy (founder of the Christian Science mother church). It's also the birthplace of Mary's little lamb, one of the Peter Rabbits (ah, the cotton tales of literary controversy), the Cat in the Hat, and the ubiquitous Kilroy. Here you will find what might be the country's oldest example of graffiti; an ancient bowling ball found in a privy; a place that always remembers the *Maine*; and museums dedicated to collections of dirt, shovels, and burnt food.

So, come meet the pirates and the healers, the artists and the ward heelers. See the house made of rolled-up newspapers, and the giant neon flag. Visit museums of plastic and of sanitary plumbing. Catch magic shows, ax murders, and lighthouse hauntings. Experience brightly painted gingerbread cottages on an island and entire towns smothered by a man-made lake. Just stifle your laughter, as the folks here can get touchy.

Massachusetts: You've got to love it. Or else.

North
Boston

Winthrop

East
Boston

(1A)

(1)

(93)

North
End

Logan
International
Airport

■Boston
Common

(90)

(93)

Boston Harbor

South Boston

GREATER BOSTON

GREATER BOSTON

THE HUB OF THE UNIVERSE
Boston

Bostonians are a self-centered lot, and why not? After all, the city's immodest nickname is The Hub as in "the hub of the universe." The phrase is actually derived from something Oliver Wendell Holmes wrote in *The Autocrat of the Breakfast-Table* about the capitol building:

> Boston State-house is the hub of the solar system. You coud n't [sic] pry that out of a Boston man if you had the tire of all creation straightened out for a crow-bar.

Since Holmes wrote this whimsical essay in 1858, the so-called center of the universe has moved a bit. You'll now find it near Filene's Basement on a spot marked with a bronze plaque about 15 feet from the store's Washington Street entrance.

The hub of the universe is in the center of a fruit market on Washington Street.
Photo by Bruce Gellerman

Perhaps fitting for its top banana status, in order to see the center of the universe, you might have to move a bunch of bananas or two . . . and perhaps some onions and a crate of oranges. The plaque, marking the hub of the universe, is now in the center of a fruit market at 426 Washington Street.

FIGHTING JOE HOOKER
Boston

A statue of Maj. Gen. Joseph "Fighting Joe" Hooker, on his mighty steed, stands in front of the entrance to the Massachusetts State House. One shudders to think what the statue might have looked like, considering what Hooker is best known for: lending his last name to the oldest profession.

Maj. Gen. Joseph Hooker lost his major battle at Chancellorsville even though he had twice as many troops as General Lee. We remember him for his activities off the battlefield.
Photo by Bruce Gellerman

Joe Hooker was a favorite son of Massachusetts. He commanded the Army of the Potomac during the Civil War, but Fighting Joe's men were a rowdy bunch and Hooker's headquarters was a den of iniquity. The encampment was said to be a combination barroom and brothel. Hooker allowed women who followed his troops to set up their tents nearby. Hence, the phrase "Hooker's Division" became the popular equivalent for prostitutes.

There is some evidence that the term "hooker" was used before the Civil War, but the story of Fighting Joe clearly was responsible for its common use today.

THE SACRED COD AND HOLY MACKEREL
Boston

Suspended over the entrance to the Massachusetts House of Representatives chamber is something you won't find hanging over any other deliberative body in the world: a cod fish. And it's not just any cod fish. It's the Sacred Cod Fish. Measuring 4 feet 11 inches, the pine carved fish is a constant reminder of the importance of the fishing industry to the state's early history. The Pilgrims and Indians feasted on cod along with turkey that first Thanksgiving, and it was the state's first export. We even named the Cape after the cod.

The fish that currently holds the place of honor above the legislative body's entry is actually the third-generation cod. The first was destroyed in a fire in 1747; the second, during the Revolutionary War. The current one has been hanging around since 1787, moved from the old statehouse to the new House chamber in 1895. It has hung there ever since, with one notable exception. In 1933 pranksters from the *Harvard Lampoon* "cod-napped" the state's seafood symbol by cutting the

The Sacred Cod.

Photo by Bruce Gellerman

The Holy Mackerel.

Photo by Bruce Gellerman

line holding it aloft, and they made off with their prize catch. Lawmakers were outraged. The state police were called in to investigate. The Charles River was dredged. Days later an anonymous tip led to the revered fish's recovery and it was hung 6 inches higher to prevent it from being stolen again.

Those who say something very fishy is going on in the Massachusetts statehouse have a basis for their claim. In 1974 the cod was elevated to the status of official state fish. Not to be outdone by the lower house, the Senate has in its chamber a wrought-iron chandelier with a fish in its design. It's called the Holy Mackerel.

Over in the House chamber, check out the second painting on the left behind the speaker's chair. It shows one of the judges from the Salem witch trials repenting for sentencing accused witches to death. The gesture is a bit late but still appreciated; after all, it's the thought that counts.

The Massachusetts State House is on Beacon Hill overlooking Boston Common on Beacon Street. Self-taught architect Charles Bullfinch designed the building, which was constructed between 1795 and 1797 on a pasture owned by John Hancock. Although it may look high now, the hill is 50 feet lower than its original height, as land from the hills was used to fill in Boston's Back Bay. The gilded dome, first made of wood shingles, is topped by a lantern and a pinecone (the latter is a symbol of the forests of Massachusetts.) The fish are indoors.

THE PARKER HOUSE HOTEL: REVOLUTIONARY ROLLS
Boston

H otels make for strange bedfellows. John Wilkes Booth, Malcolm X, Ho Chi Minh, John Crawford, Ralph Waldo

Emerson, and John F. Kennedy have all spent time at Boston's Parker House.

The hotel, now known as the Omni Parker, is the oldest continuously operated hotel in the continental United States When it opened for business in 1855, it was the first hotel in Boston to have hot and cold running water and an elevator.

John Wilkes Booth stayed here the week before he shot Abraham Lincoln. Ralph Waldo Emerson, Nathaniel Hawthorne, and Henry Wadsworth Longfellow were members of the famous literary Saturday Club, which regularly met in the hotel's restaurant. Had the wordsmiths assembled some eight decades later, Malcolm X might have cleared their table; he worked as a busboy in the hotel restaurant in 1940.

The Parker House is famous for its rolls. Legend has it that this gastronomic delight is the happy result of an angry chef. The Parker House prided itself on meeting the needs of the pickiest patron, but in 1856, when one particularly demanding guest made one too many requests for a certain roll, it is said that a hotheaded German chef began throwing small balls of dough into an oven. Surprisingly, the rolls were delicious, and the talk of delighted guests gave rise to the famed Parker House Roll. The hotel kept the recipe a secret until Pres. Franklin Roosevelt requested it in 1933.

The Boston cream pie (which is actually a cake) was also concocted here. The origin of the pie/cake is not entirely certain. Some say it was created by a French chef named Sanzian. There is no truth to the story that the misnamed dessert was part of a Communist plot to confuse American diners, although revolutionary Ho Chi Minh did work as a baker at the Parker House from 1911 to 1913.

For a taste of Old World charm, and to imagine what it must have been like way back when chefs were tossing dough and bakers were plotting coups, check out or check into the hotel at 60 School Street, (617) 227–8600. You never know who you'll meet there.

WHAT A GRAPE CATCH

I n 1988 Paul Tavilla of Arlington, Massachusetts, earned a place in the Guinness Book of Records *by catching in his mouth a grape dropped from the top of the John Hancock building, sixty stories high.*

When it comes to grape catching, what goes down obviously also goes up. The longest distance a grape has been caught after being thrown into the air from ground level is 99.82 meters—precisely 327 feet and 6 inches. That great grape catch was accomplished on May 27, 1991, by, who else, Paul Tavilla.

BOSTON IS PLANET HOLLYWOOD
Boston

B oston University is home to the largest collection of Hollywood memorabilia on the planet. The University's Department of Special Collections includes the personal papers and effects of some 2,000 luminaries of the stage and silver screen. Included in the twentieth-century archive are materials from Mary Astor, Douglas Fairbanks Jr., Marilyn Monroe, Rex Harrison, Robert Redford, and Edward G. Robinson. The Oscar

that Gene Kelly won for *An American in Paris* is on view, as
are Fred Astaire's dancing shoes and Elizabeth Taylor's gloves.

Howard Gottlieb, curator of B.U.'s Department of Special
Collections, began going through the attics and shoe boxes of
the stars in 1963. His most prized catch is 119,000 pages of
material from Bette Davis. Gottlieb called Davis twice a week
for thirty years before she agreed to donate her scripts, scrap-
books, and 5,000-volume library specializing in theater history.

In all, the archives take up 7 miles of shelves in two underground vaults. The Department of Special Collections is at 771
Commonwealth Avenue, 5th Floor. Call ahead at (617)
353–3916 if you want to see something special.

OY, YOU SHOULD ONLY LIVE SO LONG AND PROSPER

*M*r. Spock from the TV series Star Trek comes from
Vulcan via Boston. Leonard Nimoy, a.k.a. Spock,
grew up in an Orthodox Jewish household in Boston. His
religious background played a pivotal role in developing
his Vulcan character.

According to Nimoy, the idea for the Vulcan salute,
where four fingers of each hand are split, comes from a
boyhood lesson he learned at temple. The gesture creates
the Hebrew letter shin, representing the first letter of the
Almighty and the word peace. Nimoy proposed the hand
signal when the producers of the show were trying to
come up with a salute for his character.

CAN YOU IMAGINE HOW BIG THE TEA BAG IS?
Boston

I t is only right and proper that the city where the most famous tea party in history took place would have the world's largest tea kettle. The giant pot was cast in 1873 and it hung over the Oriental Teashop until 1967, when it was moved

Tea for two . . . two thousand, that is. The giant teapot in Boston's City Hall Plaza has been spouting steam since 1873.
Photo by Bruce Gellerman

just a few doors down the street to its present site. The kettle
holds precisely 227 gallons, 2 quarts, 1 pint, and 3 gills and
blows steam through its spout.

Ironically, the kettle now hangs above a Starbucks store at
63 Court Street, near the Government Center metro station.
Perhaps if the java chain had been around in 1773 we'd be calling it the "Boston Coffee Klatch" today.

JFK ATE HERE
Boston

O bviously, John F. Kennedy ate at a lot of places in his hometown. One of his favorites was the Union Oyster House,
where the Kennedy clan dined regularly on the restaurant's
namesake mollusk. In the private upstairs dining room, you
will find a plaque on Kennedy's favorite booth, number 18, dedicated to his memory in 1977.

Kennedy was just one of many Harvard students to fre-
quent the restaurant. Supposedly, some were paid to eat there.
Oyster House lore has it that an importer of toothpicks from
South America hired Harvard students to dine at the restaurant and request the picks as a way to boost sales.

The Union Oyster House is located at 41 Union Street. To
request a table or JFK's favorite booth, call (617) 227–2750.

LET THEM EAT SANDWICHES!

B oston's first public playground was a sand-
box. The sand garden, as it was called in
those days, was built in 1886 by the philanthropic women of the North End Union. It was
created to serve the needs of immigrant Italian,
Irish, and Jewish children in the area.

At the time, Kate Gannet Wells of the philanthropic committee said, "Playing in the dirt is
the royalty of childhood."

The site at 20 Parmenter Street is across the
street from the North End branch of the Boston
Public Library, where you will find a diorama
of the Ducal Palace of Venice made by local
artist Louise Stimson in 1949.

GOT MILK?
Boston

The Hood Milk Bottle, near the Children's Museum at 300 Congress Street, is a pint-sized display—400,000 pints, that is, or 50,000 gallons, in case your math has gone sour. Either way, it would give you a giant milk mustache. The wooden bottle is 40 feet high and was built in 1938. During the summer it also serves as an ice cream stand and snack bar.

Milk with your tea? The giant Hood Milk Bottle
stands near the site of the Boston Tea Party.
Photo by Bruce Gellerman

THE BOSTON UNIVERSITY BRIDGE

*B*ostonians will tell you that the Boston University Bridge crossing the Charles River is the only bridge in the world where an airplane can fly over a person riding a bicycle, next to a car, going over a train, that's traveling over a boat. It's true—that is, if you don't count the Brooklyn Bridge, where the train (a subway in a tunnel) goes under the boat.

I'LL HAVE A VERY SHORT ONE: THE LITTLEST BAR
Boston

Without a doubt, Boston's most famous watering hole is the one from TV fame: the Cheers bar. Two establishments bearing this name cater to the tourist trade. One is at 84 Beacon Street and the other is in Faneuil Market. It's unlikely that anyone at either place will know your name, so if you want recognition and a little something to drink, take a short walk across Boston Public Garden to 47 Providence Street. The bar

For a wee bit of blarney, check out the tiny
basement pub the Littlest Bar.
Photo by Bruce Gellerman

there is so cozy that everyone will quickly learn your name. It's the smallest bar in Boston, appropriately named the Littlest Bar. Built in 1945, the Littlest is a wee small subterranean Irish pub just 16 feet wide and 22 feet long, seating just 38 patrons. Leprechauns would love it.

Don't forget to check out the minuscule bathroom. There you will find a plaque commemorating Irish Nobel Prize-winning novelist Seamus Heaney. It says, "SEAMUS HEANEY PEED HERE." Now there's something you won't see at Cheers. To find out if there's room for you, call (617) 523-9766.

A Clean Get-Away,
Except for the Smell

On January 17, 1950, robbers broke into the Brinks offices at 169 Prince Street in Boston's North End. They made off with $1,218,211.29 in cash and $1,557,183.83 in securities and checks. The Great Brinks Robbery was the biggest heist in U.S. history. It took six years and $29 million for the government to find and prosecute the crooks. Only $51,906 of the Brinks cash was ever recovered. A big breakthrough in the case came when one of the robbers tried to pass off money that he had hidden in the dirt. The buried loot became smelly and moldy and led to the case being cracked.

The building where thieves pulled off the Great Brinks Robbery still stands and is now known as the North Terminal Garage. It is on the National Register of Historic Places. The address is 600 Commercial Avenue.

The building where the famous Brinks
job was pulled off made for a speedy
getaway: All four floors have direct
access to ground level.
Photo by Bruce Gellerman

THE CHRISTMAS TREE IS THE PRESENT
Boston

If you want to see the most magnificent Christmas tree in the nation, forget about the ones at the White House and New York's Rockefeller Center. They dim in comparison to the one in Boston. For more than thirty years, Boston's official Christmas tree in Boston Common has run rings around any and all competitors. But don't take our word for it. The seasonal symbol comes from Nova Scotia, Canada, the self-proclaimed "Christmas Tree Capital of the World," as an annual gift selected after a six-month search. By tradition, the tree has to be at least fifty years old and 50 feet tall.

Why all the hubbub over the Hub's tree? It's a show of gratitude for the help Boston sent to Halifax during its time of greatest need. In early December 1917 a ship filled with munitions exploded in Halifax harbor. It was the largest artificially created explosion in history until the detonation of the atomic bomb. Halifax was flattened; thousands were killed and injured. Boston citizens braved a blizzard to deliver food, medical aid, and supplies to the city, and Halifax has never forgotten.

The traditional lighting of Boston's official Christmas tree takes place in early December in Boston Common.

WHAT'S UP, DUCK?
Boston

R obert McCloskey's *Make Way for Ducklings* is Massachusetts's official children's book. The children's classic features Mr. and Mrs. Mallard's darling little ducklings: Jack, Kack, Lack, Mack, Nack, Ouack, Quack, and Pack.

After being "duck-napped," Jack the duckling is back on his feet.
Photo by Bruce Gellerman

A 38-foot-long bronze sculpture of the jaywalking ducklings and their mom can be found in the northeast corner of
Boston's Public Garden. The statue, sculpted by Nancy Schon,
was installed in 1987 and quickly became a favorite of residents and visitors alike. Then in 1999 someone "duck-napped"
Jack. Bostonians, usually unflappable about such matters, were
incensed. Thankfully, a month later the statue was found
under a desk at a Boston college. But the duck-napper had
sawed Jack's legs off just above his webbed feet, so a new Jack
had to be made. The one in Boston Garden is the new Jack. The
old Jack, with his legs repaired, now has a new home at the
rooftop playground outside Boston Medical Center's pediatric
department at 84 Harrison Avenue.

A DEATH-DEFYING COLONIAL DAREDEVIL
Boston

One if by land, two if by sea. Three if by air? Boston's Old
North Church, perhaps best known as the place where Paul
Revere got the signal that set him off on his midnight ride,
also happens to be where colonial stuntman John Childs took
the first flight in Boston history.

In 1757, eighteen years before Revere got his signal, John
Childs used the church steeple as a launching pad. A plaque on
a wall outside the Old North Church describes how Childs flew
from the 190-foot steeple "to the satisfaction of a great number
of spectators."

There are two versions of the event. One has Childs strap-
ping on a leather umbrella-like contraption, putting a grooved
wooden board on his chest, and sliding headfirst down a 700-
foot-long guyline. The other version has him wearing canvas
wings and gliding down. Either way, the colonial daredevil

drew such a large crowd that he did it again the next day while shooting off pistols. The performance proved too much for Boston's Puritan prudes. They banned all future flights of fantasy, a prohibition on aviation that stands on the city's books to this day.

The plaque commemorating Childs's flight is the third from the left on the brick Washington Garden wall near the main entrance to the Old North Church, 193 Salem Street.

ONCE UPON A MIDNIGHT FROGPONDIUM

*A*lthough Edgar Allen Poe pondered weak and weary and died in Baltimore, the master of the macabre was born in Boston in 1809. Orphaned as a child, Poe lived in Boston only a short time, returning briefly in 1827 when he enlisted in the U.S. Army under the name Edgar A. Perry. While Poe was in Boston his first book of poems, Tamerlane and other Poems, was published, written anonymously "by a Bostonian." Poe had a love–hate relationship with Boston and may have been reluctant to have his name attached to the city of his birth; he often referred to Boston as "Frogpondium" after the frog pond on the Common.

Perhaps appropriately, Poe's exact birthplace is in dispute. Some put it at 33 Hollis Street; others say it was on Carver Street, which is now called Charles Street South. To avoid the dispute, the plaque honoring Poe is near 176 Boylston Street.

THE NUMBER 576

The colorful, charismatic, and corrupt James Michael Curley was the first mayor of Boston to have an automobile. His license plate, 576, represented the number of letters in his first, middle, and last names. The same sequence was used by every mayor of the city until 1993, when Thomas Menino decided to lease a car to save the city money. (How times have changed.)

Curley not only served as mayor of Boston, governor of the state, and congressman; he also served two terms in jail, for misuse of federal funds and for taking a civil service exam for a friend. Neither time was his prison number 576.

HEY NORTON, CHECK THIS OUT
Boston

You can never tell what you'll find when you spend $14.5 billion and dig through 16 million cubic yards of dirt.

Archaeologists working alongside excavators on Boston's Big Dig, the largest public works project in history, have unearthed the usual arrowheads, some clay tobacco pipes, and the oldest bowling ball in North America. If that doesn't bowl you over, perhaps this will: They found the ball under the floor-boards in a "house of office," the seventeenth-century term for a privy.

The oak ball is flattened on two sides and is about the size of a grapefruit. It has a perforated middle to hold a lead weight to give the ball more play when rolled. Not that play was what the Puritans had in mind when they founded Boston: A statute forbidding bowling was passed in 1646 because it caused "much waste of wine and beer."

Perhaps a bowler taking a nip too much might explain why the ball was found in the toilet.

Today the oldest bowling ball in North America is on display at the Commonwealth Museum, 220 Morissey. Admission is free but you'll have to pay for shoes.

For more information, call (617) 727–9268 or visit www .state.ma.us/sec/mus.

AN AIRPORT NAMED FOR A VERY INFREQUENT FLIER

*B*oston's Logan International Airport, one of the busiest in the nation, is named in honor of Lt. Gen. Edward Lawrence Logan. Logan was born in Boston in 1875 and led a distinguished career as an elected official, judge, and war hero. He died in 1929.

The question is: Why did they name an airport after him? For all of his many accomplishments, Lieutenant General Logan never flew in an airplane.

THE RUNNING OF
THE BRIDES

*F*ilene's Basement's notorious bridal gown event has
been likened to the running of the bulls at Pam-
plona. But according to the store's PR person, Pat
Boudrot, some years it's more like a prize fight, as
brides-to-be go head-to-head in an attempt to grab a
designer wedding gown at a bargain-basement $249.

Some of the women arrive with retinues that include
their moms and matrons of honor, ready to do battle.
Boudrot says they come wearing boxing gloves and
chomping on mouth guards. It's a knock-down, no-holds-
or clothes-barred fight to the finish as the gals make a
mad dash for the dresses, stripping themselves and the
racks bare in just seconds. The record, witnessed by a
CBS news camera team, is just 36 seconds. It's a scene
that makes the floor of the New York Stock Exchange
look like, well, a walk down the aisle.

Filene's Basement first emptied its warehouse of
designer gowns for the one-day sale in 1947. Since then,
on at least five occasions, starry eyed women, with their
sights set on a "baaaahhhhgain" have broken down the
doors to the store before they were opened.

The objects of their affections are dresses that come
from manufacturers' overstocks, cancelled store orders,
and, of course, cancelled weddings. The gowns may retail
for up to $10,000 and sell for as low as $199 on this one
lucky day. One memorable gown featured
a peacock hand-painted in pas-
tels; another had a map of
the world laid out in
Mercator projection on
the skirt.

Marketing professors Ellen Foxman and Susan Dobscha have made a cottage industry of writing scholarly papers about the sale. Their latest, "Women and Wedding Gowns: Exploring a Discount Shopping Experience," is in the proceedings of the 1998 Conference on Gender, Marketing, and Consumer Behavior.

Filene's Basement has expanded the sale to many of its stores around the nation, but the one in the original store at Boston's Downtown Crossing is the first and still the most frenetic.

Brides strip the racks and themselves bare at Filene's Basement Bridal Gown Sale.
Photo courtesy of Filene's Basement

THE SACCO AND VANZETTI
DEATH MASKS
Boston

There are many proud moments in Massachusetts's history, but August 23, 1927, is not one of them. That was the day when Italian immigrants Nicola Sacco, a shoemaker from Stoughton, and Bartolomeo Vanzetti, a fisherman from North Plymouth, were executed on the site that is now part of Bunker Hill Community College in Boston.

The men, followers of Italy's most radical anarchist, were found guilty of armed robbery and murder. Both men denied the charges up to their deaths. The evidence against the men was weak and circumstantial and their executions ignited protests around the world. The case became a landmark in the judicial history of the state and nation. Fifty years to the day of their execution, Massachusetts governor Michael Dukakis issued a proclamation apologizing to the men and their families.

Copies of Sacco's and Vanzetti's death certificates are housed in the rare books department of the Boston Public Library, along with a canister of their ashes, their death masks, a box of bullets, and other personal items. Boston Public Library is at Copley Square.

Visitors are asked to e-mail ahead of time so that the materials can be accessed. Write to rzonghi@bpl.org.

The Boston Public Library's special collections also contain more than over 700 anarchist newspapers and periodicals from around the world.

HOW SWEET IT ISN'T

*A*bout half past noon on January 15, 1919, a disaster like no other struck Boston's North End. A giant concrete-and-cast-iron tank, 52 feet high and 90 feet in diameter and holding 2.3 million gallons of molasses, exploded. The powerful blast propelled a gooey, 2-story tidal wave down Commercial Avenue at thirty-five miles an hour. Steel supports for a nearby elevated train line were severed and a fire station was crushed. Twenty-one people were killed, 150 were injured, and an untold number of horses drowned in the steaming, sweet lava. Left in its wake was a 2-foot layer of molasses that had spread for blocks. Cleanup crews and sightseers brought it on their shoes and clothes all over Boston and as far away as Worcester. While the sickly, sweet smell allegedly lingered for decades, there's not a trace of the molasses today. Not even a plaque marks the spot where the doomed tank once stood, but if you look down from Copp's Hill onto Commercial Avenue, you'll see a park next to an enclosed recreation center. That's the place.

TANKS VERMILION,
HO HO HO CHI MINH
Boston

The world's largest copyrighted work of art is on permanent display just south of Boston in Dorcester on Route 93. It's the so-called Rainbow Tank, a 140-foot-tall liquid natural gas tank featuring five huge stripes of color: vermilion, orange, yellow, blue, and purple.

In 1971 Boston Gas commissioned artist Corita Kent to paint the tank. Kent, a former nun best known for designing the famous LOVE postage stamp, said the Rainbow Tank was an expression of peace. The war in Vietnam was raging, and Kent was a peace activist. Some say they can see evidence of Kent's anti-war sympathies hidden in the tank. Look at the middle stripe. See the profile of Ho Chi Minh? Who? Ho Chi Minh, the former leader of North Vietnam and a busboy at Boston's Parker House Hotel in the 1920s. Others say the roadside Rorschach test contains the image of the devil, Osama Bin Laden, or Fred Flintstone. And then there are those who say that sometimes a tank is just a tank.

Be careful: Don't use the access road leading to the tank. It's private property. There are remote cameras watching you and the property owners will call the police if you are on the road.

*The gas tank along Interstate 93 is a roadside
Rorschach test. Some people say they see Ho Chi
Minh's profile painted on the tank.*
Photo by Erik Sherman

YOU DEFINITELY SAVE
ON WALL-TO-WALL CARPET
Boston

Jennifer Simonic; her husband, Spence Welton; their daughter; and their dog and cat live at 44 Hull Street in Boston's North End. This 200-year-old, four-story town house has been beautifully restored, but it is easy to miss. The house is just 10 feet 5 inches wide. The home is so narrow that the front door is located on the side. The ceilings are 6 feet 4 inches high. (Spence Welton is 6 feet 1 inch tall.)

The Skinny House, as it is called, is the narrowest home in Boston—if not the entire commonwealth. Legend has it that the house was built out of spite to block the view of neighbors behind it. Admittedly, that's a pretty thin story. More likely, it is the last of a series of similar homes built in the area around 1800. At one time eleven people lived in the house. Ironically, the Skinny House has a spacious, 1,000-square-foot backyard, one of the largest in the densely populated North End.

The Skinny House is located directly opposite Copp's Hill Burying Ground. The house number is on the side.

The house at 44 Hull Street in Boston is the
skinniest house in the city, and perhaps in the
entire commonwealth.
Photo by Bruce Gellerman

ETHER OR EITHER
Boston

Boston printer Gilbert Allen never knew what hit him. After a few whiffs from an ether-soaked sponge, he was out. When he woke up, the human guinea pig learned he had made medical history. It was October 16, 1846, and Gilbert Allen was the first person to be successfully operated on while under anesthesia. Before then, undergoing an operation had meant enduring excruciating pain. Now, the ether-assisted surgery proceeded in silence as an astonished crowd of physicians looked on. Afterward, Dr. John Warren, the surgeon who performed the operation, told his incredulous colleagues, "Gentleman, this is no humbug."

Bah, humbug, indeed. The operation touched off a controversy of competing claims over who actually had invented the potent stuff, with two Boston dentists taking credit. When city authorities proposed a monument memorializing the inventor, they consulted Harvard physician and wordsmith Oliver Wendell Holmes. It was Holmes who coined the term *anesthesia* and, acting Solomon-like, suggested dedicating the statue to "Either or ether."

When Mark Twain learned that neither man would be named on the statue, he proclaimed that the ether monument "is made of hardy material, but the lie it tells will outlast it a million years." Well, either it will or ether it won't, but it has lasted since its unveiling in 1868 in Boston Common. It is the oldest monument in the country's oldest public park. The Ether Memorial can be found facing Arlington Street. Atop the red marble columns is a rendition of the Good Samaritan. Be sure to check out the weird reliefs behind the granite arches.

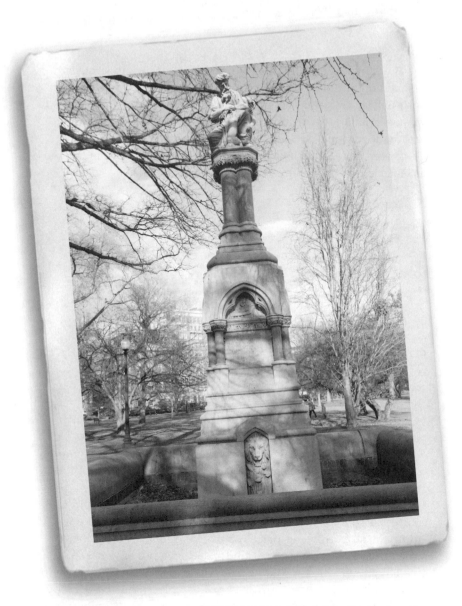

Patients breathed a lot easier after the invention
of ether. This monument in Boston Garden pays
homage to the pain-killing gas.
Photo by Erik Sherman

The surgical amphitheater in which the first anesthesia-assisted operation took place is called the Ether Dome. It was designed by the great architect Charles Bullfinch. Until 1873 it was used as an operating room. Then it served as a storage area, a dormitory, and a dining room for nurses. It is now a classroom. The Ether Dome is open to the public and is located at Massachusetts General Hospital, 55 Fruit Street.

THE GARDNER MUSEUM: WHAT YOU DON'T SEE IS WHAT YOU GET
Boston

The magnificent Isabella Stewart Gardner Museum contains an eclectic collection of 2,500 paintings, sculptures, tapestries, pieces of furniture, manuscripts, and rare books. Mrs. Gardner, the grande dame of Boston's Brahmin high society, spent thirty years assembling the renowned collection and built a fifteenth-century Venetian palace with courtyard garden to house it.

But today what makes the collection a must-see for many tourists is what you do not see, as evidenced by the empty frames that hang on the walls. On St. Patrick's Day 1990, the Gardner Museum was the scene of the biggest art heist in U.S. history. Two men wearing fake mustaches and Boston Police uniforms stole thirteen priceless works of art. Among them were three Rembrandts (including the master's only seascape), five Degas sketches, a Manet, and Vermeer's *The Concert.* Despite a $5-million reward, none of the pieces has been recovered. The empty frames continue to hang on the walls because Mrs. Gardner stipulated in her will that everything in the house was forever to remain exactly as it was or all her possessions would pass to Harvard University.

The Isabella Stewart Gardner Museum is located at 280 The
Fenway. For more information, call (617) 566–1401 or visit
www.gardnermuseum.org. The Gardner is closed on most
major holidays and usually on St. Patrick's Day.

GILLETTE EMPLOYEES GET WORKED UP INTO A LATHER
Boston

B ack in 1901 traveling salesman King Camp Gillette developed the world's first double-edged disposable blade, and the
hirsute have never been the same. Today, from its World Shaving Headquarters in South Boston, where Gillette founded his
international empire, the company turns out blades by the billions. To ensure that the company lives up to its claim that
Gillette's razors are "the best a man can get" and that they get
even better, Gillette employs 500 engineers and scientists in
laboratories around the world who send their improvements
back to Boston for evaluation.

More than 300 volunteers at the South Boston factory sign
up for the shave-in-plant program to test-drive the latest exper-
imental models. Each morning a select group of men take off
their shirts, enter one of twenty booths, and lather up. Techni-
cians in white lab coats register their reactions as the men
shave the right side of their faces with one unmarked razor
and the left side with another. The results are entered into a
computer. After decades of studying shaving and blades under
electron microscopes and in slow motion, Gillette has come to
understand that making a blade shave smoother than a baby's
bottom takes a lot more than science and technology. Because
it sells blades from Armenia to Zanzibar, Gillette has to be

sensitive to the different kinds of skin and hair types, and to cultural differences as well. Over the years, shaving scientists have learned that what constitutes a great shave is really a subjective experience; there's the sound of the blade slicing through whiskers, the feel of the razor in the hand. After all the testing and experimenting, it turns out that when it comes to shaving, beauty is in the eye of the beard holder.

YOU NEED THIS MUSEUM LIKE A HOLE IN THE HEAD

Boston

T he Warren Anatomical Museum is the kind of place to which Alfred Hitchcock might have brought a first date. The museum is fascinating in a macabre sort of way, and not without humor, with a vast collection of medical instruments, photos, anatomical models, machines, gadgets, specimens, body parts, and medical memorabilia. In all, more than 13,000 arti-facts detail the evolution of modern medical science from the nineteenth to the twentieth century. You'll be astonished by how far medicine has come in such a short period of time . . . and perhaps be unnerved by just how primitive it was until not too long ago.

Dr. John Collin Warren started collecting unusual anatomi-cal specimens in 1799, when he was just twelve years old. In 1848 he hung up his stethoscope (there are scores of models on display) and resigned his Harvard professorship, donating his world-class collection of weird artifacts to the medical school. His own skeleton is now part of the collection.

On display is the phrenological collection of Dr. Johann Gaspar Spurzheim, who studied skull bumps for clues about personality and brain function. In 1832 the famed German doctor died unexpectedly in Boston while on a lecture tour. His body is buried in Mount Auburn Cemetery in Cambridge, but his unusually large skull is on display at the Warren Museum.

The most popular exhibit is the skull of Phineas Gage. An on-the-job accident sent a thirteen-pound steel bar flying through Gage's cheek into his brain. Unexpectedly, Gage survived. His memory was intact but his personality took a turn for the worse. He became mean and lost his social constraints. Scientists studied Gage's skull for clues about personality. Seems they needed just such an accident, like a hole in the head, to discover the inner workings of the brain.

The Warren Anatomical Museum Exhibition Gallery is on the fifth floor of the Countway Library of Medicine, 10 Shattuck Street; (617) 432–6196.

Spurzheim Tomb is at the intersection of Fountain and Lawn Avenues, left sides, adjacent to the road in Mount Auburn Cemetery, Mount Auburn Street, Cambridge. Watch out for the bumps in the road.

AMERICANS "IN-VEST" IN AN INSECT
Boston

Since 1742, a 52-inch-tall, 38-pound copper grasshopper with glass doorknob eyes has looked down onto a good deal of American history. The 'hopper has watched from his weathervane perch 80 feet above the ground as the winds of change turned the colonies into a nation and the nation into a world superpower. From the grasshopper's vantage point atop Faneuil Hall, the insect has been an eyewitness to the Boston Massacre and the Boston Tea Party and watched as patriotic conspirators gathered at the Old Meeting House. Over time the grasshopper has survived wars, hurricanes, earthquakes, fires, and vandals.

But the statue is more than a priceless piece of Americana. The grasshopper is also a time capsule. Inside the insect's stomach vest area is a copper container. Each time the grasshopper has been handled and restored, people have placed objects into the vest and taken things out.

In 1761, following a devastating fire and an earthquake, a note inscribed "food for the Grasshopper" was inserted into the copper time capsule by the restorer. The note, detailing the gilded insect's trials and tribulations, is now in the Boston Public Library's archives.

In 1842 the weather vane was restored again. This time it was filled with papers and coins. It is believed that the first contents were removed and sold at auction in 1885. In 1889 some newspapers and coins from the period were deposited in the capsule, and in 1952 Boston's mayor inserted one of his business cards and a message in the copper vest.

In 1974 the grasshopper was reported missing and a massive insect hunt was started.

The 'hopper was discovered weeks later in the Faneuil Hall belfry underneath a pile of old flags. Seems painters had taken it down and forgot to put it back up. A tip from an ex-steeplejack who worked on the vane and was trying to beat a drug rap led to its recovery. Before the grasshopper was restored to its proper perch, Boston's mayor resealed all of the items in the vest, adding a letter of his own and two bicentennial coins.

The third floor of Faneuil Hall still houses the Ancient and Honorable Artillery Company. Founded in 1638, this is the oldest military company in the United States, and considered the third oldest in the world. Among its collection is one of the grasshopper's eye sockets. The Hall is adjacent to Quincy Market.

NOW, WHERE DID I PUT THAT KEY?
Boston

The giant Fortress padlock is a familiar, neck-bending icon for motorists on Interstate 93. When fully inflated, the 700-pound lock is 32 feet tall and 20 feet wide. To make sure the blow-up lock doesn't blow away, it's taken down for the winter and stored—where else?—in the super-secure, climate-controlled Fortress storage facility.

The giant padlock can be seen from Interstate 93, just south of Boston.
Photo courtesy of the Fortress Corporation

The eight-story Fortress building at 99 Boston Street is also unique. Fortress, the largest provider of high-security storage in the United States, invented a giant carousel device that suspends the room-sized safety deposit vaults in midair and automatically delivers them to clients waiting in the lobby. The giant lock is in good company. Many museums use Fortress to store their works of art.

A Thin Tome from the Tomb
Boston

James Allen's autobiography is one book you can definitely judge by its cover. It is awful, inside and out. Allen admits he was a rotten scoundrel, and the book cover testifies to that. His autobiography is certainly him; the book is bound in his skin.

In 1833 Allen attempted to rob John Fenno Jr. near Powderhorn Hill in Chelsea. Fenno fought back and was shot, but he survived because Allen's bullet hit the buckle on Fenno's suspenders. Allen was arrested and sent to prison, where he wrote an autobiography of his troubled youth and his life as a highwayman.

Allen died on July 17, 1837, but before he did he asked to meet with Fenno, saying he wanted to shake the hand of a brave man. Then he made his fateful request. Figuring that once he was dead it would be no skin off his nose—or actually his back—Allen asked that a copy of his autobiography, bound in his skin, be given to Fenno and a second copy be given to Dr. Bigelow of Boston, the physician he requested attend his death.

Allen's skin was removed and bookbinder Peter Low tanned his hide and edged it in gold. The binding looks like pale gray deerskin and is inscribed in Latin: *Hic Liber Waltonis cute Compactus Est* ("This book by Walton bound in his own skin").

Binding his autobiography was no skin off James Allen's nose.
The cover came from his back. Photo by Bruce Gellerman

The full title of the book is: *Narrative of the life of James Allen,*
alias George Walton, alias Jonas Pierce, alias James H. York,
alias Burley Grove, the highwayman. Being his death-bed
confession, to the warden of the Massachusetts state prison.

Allen's autobiography was donated to the Boston
Athenaeum by one of John Fenno's descendants and you can
still find it there today, but the copy given to the doctor has
never been found. The Boston Athenaeum (617–227–0270) is
located at an address Harry Potter would love: 10½ Beacon
Street in Boston.

The Athenaeum's collection includes 600,000 volumes.
James Allen's autobiography is the one most often requested.
You can access the text of the thin tome on the Athenaeum's
Web site at www.bostonathenaeum.org.

Bridges That "Lie" Over Waters

*A*s far as we're concerned it's all water under the bridge, but just to set the record straight, the Boston guidebooks have it wrong. Despite what they say, the iron bridge that crosses the swan lagoon in Boston's Public Garden is not the world's smallest suspension bridge. When it was built in 1866, the span, a quaint fifty-six paces long, was indeed a suspension bridge, but repairs in the early 1900s turned it into a plain old bridge.

Boston's newest bridge, the Leonard P. Zakim Bunker Hill Bridge, emerging from the underground Central Artery near Causeway Street, may also look like a suspension job, but it's not. It's a cable-stayed bridge. In fact, it's the widest cable-stayed bridge in the world. Both a suspension bridge and a cable-stayed bridge use two towers, but there is a difference in how the cables are attached to the towers. In a cable-stayed bridge, the cables run directly between the roadbed and the towers, and the towers bear the load. Suspension bridges have the cables slung over the towers, and they transfer the load to the anchorages on the other side.

While you are trying to figure out the difference, check out the new bridge's towers. They look just like the Bunker Hill Memorial to the east. The bridge is named after the famous battle and for Lenny Zakim, a Jewish activist who tried to bridge the difference of Boston's many racial, religious, and ethnic communities. For his work, Zakim was even named Knight of St. Gregory by Pope John Paul II in 1999.

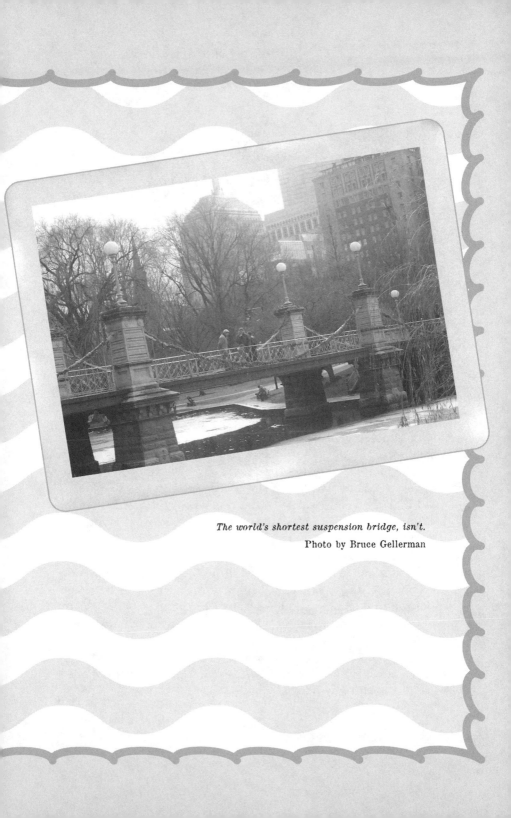

The world's shortest suspension bridge, isn't.

Photo by Bruce Gellerman

THE PLYWOOD PALACE
Boston

Building the sixty-story John Hancock Tower, Boston's tallest skyscraper, was a real "pane in the glass." In 1973, soon after workmen began installing the first of 10,344 windows, the panes began to crack and many of the windows fell to the ground. Luckily, no one was killed or injured.

The entire exterior of the 790-foot building had been designed to be covered in special mirror-glass, but by April 1973 plywood had replaced more than an acre of the tower's high-tech windows. The building became known as the Plywood Palace.

Needless to say, lawyers had a field day—or, in this case, field years. There were lawsuits and countersuits and counter-countersuits. Scientists and engineers were perplexed. After much high-tech sleuthing, the problem was identified. However, the judge in the case imposed a gag order on the aggrieved parties that lasted seventeen years. It was not until 1990 that the public learned what was wrong. It seems that the bonding material that was supposed to hold the dual layers of insulated glass together, didn't.

All 10,344 windows were replaced with single sheets of tempered glass. Sensors were installed on each pane to provide an early warning if any pane began vibrating too much. Five thousand undamaged windows were sold to the public for $100 each. As for the plywood? It was used to board up abandoned buildings in the city.

The Hancock Tower is located on Clarendon Street and St. James Place near Copley Square. You can't miss it. It's the one with all the shiny windows.

The Hancock building was dubbed the Plywood
Palace after workers replaced fallen windows
with sheets of wood.
Photo courtesy of Peter Vanderwarker

"THE BRITISH ARE COMING. OPEN WIDE. THE BRITISH ARE COMING. BITE DOWN."

*T*rying to get sleepy colonists awake and aware that the British were coming must have been like pulling teeth for Paul Revere. It's a good thing, then, that our alarmist, patriotic midnight rider wasn't only a highly skilled silversmith but talented in the art of oral health and hygiene. On August 20, 1770, five years before his midnight ride, Revere took out this ad in the Boston Gazette and Country Journal:

> *Paul Revere Takes this Method of returning his most sincere Thanks to the Gentlemen and Ladies who have employed him in the care of their Teeth. He would now inform them and all others, who are so unfortunate as to lose their Teeth by accident or otherways, that he still continues the Business of a Dentist, and flatters himself that from the Experience he has had these Two Years (in which Time he has fixt some Hundreds of Teeth) that he can fix them as well as any Surgeon-Dentist who ever came from London. He fixes them in such a Manner that they are not only an Ornament, but of real Use in Speaking and Eating. He cleanses the Teeth and will wait on any Gentleman or Lady at their Lodgings. He may be spoke with at his Shop opposite Dr. Clark's at the North End.*

CURIOSITY OF THE MONTH
Boston

When Jeremy Belknap founded the Massachusetts Historical Society in 1791, he asked the public to submit unusual contributions to the organization's collection. Since then, the Society's "curiosity collection" has grown to hold some very unusual artifacts including a five-dollar bill featuring Santa Claus, issued in 1850 by the Howard Banking Company (it was legal tender back then); a letter from Boston native Benjamin Franklin describing his attempt to electrocute a turkey; and a World Series medal from the 1912 Boston Red Sox. Little is known about the medal, but it is obviously very rare. The last time the Red Sox won the series was in 1918, the year they traded Babe Ruth to the New York Yankees and so began "the curse of the Bambino."

The Massachusetts Historical Society is at 1154 Boylston Street, (617) 536–1608. The Society maintains an "object of the month" online showcase of some of its more unusual artifacts at www.masshist.org/welcome.

FINDING BERT COHEN'S MARBLES
Boston

Bertram Cohen readily admits he's crazy about his hobby, but obviously he hasn't lost his marbles. In fact, he had 300,000 at last count. In his Victorian town house in Boston's Back Bay,

Bert Cohen has all his marbles . . . and then some.
Photo by Bruce Gellerman

Cohen has amassed what just might be the largest collection of marbles in the world. They fill his basement, hallways, and a study; they're in bags and bins, buckets and barrels. He's got onion skins, Joseph's coats, sulfides, immies, aggies, and, of course, cat's eyes. The marbles are everywhere, along with a huge collection of books about the history and playing of the game and assorted historic photos and marble memorabilia.

Bert has been a marble consultant and historian for more than forty years, collecting, swapping, and selling marbles large and small, old and new. His largest marble is a custom-made job that rolls in at thirty-three pounds; the smallest is just one-sixteenth of an inch in diameter. One of his most unusual and valuable marbles is 4,000 years old, which is kid stuff when you consider that the game goes back 10,000 years.

Bert doesn't play anymore himself; but he does give out mass-produced marbles by the shovelful to worthy causes, such as the Boy Scouts. He gets them from a factory in Mexico that churns out fifteen million a day. Collectors who share Bert's mania for marbles gather at an annual event he has organized for the past quarter-century in Marlborough.

Now, having the world's largest collection of marbles might be enough for some people, but not for Bert Cohen. He's an admitted pack rat and also has an extensive collection of glass-ware and what certainly must be the largest, if not only, collec-tion of toys made by the long-gone Irving Corporation, maker of some of the first plastic toys.

Visits to Bertram Cohen's marble museum and toy empo-rium are by special invitation only, but you can learn more about his marbles at his Web site at www.marblebert.com/publications.htm.

SIGNS OF THE TIMES
Boston

Soaring 200 feet high over Kenmore Square, seemingly float-ing in midair, is one of Boston's more obvious and beloved landmarks: the Citgo sign. Built by City Services Oil Company in 1965, the giant ad—60 by 60 feet—glows orange, red, and white from 5,878 neon tubes.

The Citgo sign sits atop 660 Beacon Street in Kenmore
Square. The building, originally known as the Peerless
Motor Car Building, now houses a bookstore.
Photo by Bruce Gellerman

Appropriately enough, the brightly lit sign is located on
Beacon Street and is used by Bostonians to orient themselves
around the city. However, in 1973 residents wandered around
confused and directionless when the lights were turned off for a
year as a symbol of conservation during the energy crisis. Then
from 1979 to 1982 there were again lost souls in the streets
when the sign was turned off once more to save electricity.

Just how important the Citgo sign had become to residents became clear in November 1982, when workers arrived to dismantle the sign. Before they could remove a single bulb, the Boston Landmark Commission intervened, saying the sign was a "prime example of roadside culture." There was talk of designating the sign an official city landmark, but Citgo would have had to pay to move it. Instead, the company paid $450,000 to refurbish the sign and return it to its original glow. On August 10, 1983, as the song "You Light Up My Life" filled the air in Kenmore Square, 750 people attended the relighting ceremony. Today the beloved Citgo sign is as much a part of Boston as the Old Meeting House or Faneuil Hall, and they don't have a single neon tube.

LADY MADONNA
East Boston

Not far from Suffolk Downs Racetrack and overlooking Logan Airport is the Madonna, Queen of the Universe National Shrine. The 35-foot bronze-and-copper statue was created by Italian–Jewish sculptor Arrigo Minerbi and set on the site in 1954.

Driving up the winding road to the shrine, you will see a 50-foot cross atop a hill. The hill is where the second battle of the American Revolution was fought. The views of Boston and the airport from the top of the hill are terrific. A gift shop near the shrine offers unusual religious object for sale.

The Madonna, Queen of the Universe National Shrine (617–569–2100) is at 111 Orient Avenue, East Boston. Follow the signs on Route 1A.

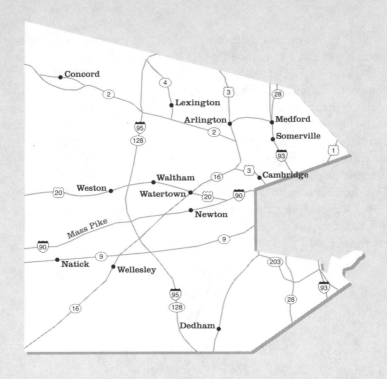

THE TECHNOLOGY RING AROUND BOSTON

THE TECHNOLOGY RING AROUND BOSTON

A WELL-DONE MUSEUM
Arlington

Where there's smoke, there's Deborah Henson-Conant. Put a harp in her hands and boy, can she cook! With her long beaded hair and leather halter top, she plays the heaven-sent instrument with the fire of a bat out of . . . well, you-know-where.

Doc Severinson calls Henson-Conant a wild woman of the harp, serving up blues, jazz, Celtic, and folk music with a generous serving of humor. But put her in the kitchen of her Arlington, Massachusetts, home and the menu changes dramatically.

Henson-Conant is the founder of (and curator, and primary contributor to) the Museum of Burnt Food, an ever-expanding collection that celebrates the art of culinary disaster. Sometime in 1989, while heating a pot of apple cider on her stove, she was distracted from her task by a lengthy telephone call. By the time she returned, the cider had turned to cinder (exhibit A). She proudly mounted and displayed the piece and, voila, the Museum of Burnt Food was born. The Museum's motto: "To cook the museum way—always leave the flame on low . . . and then take a long nap."

For a meal Smokey Bear might love, check out
the Museum of Burnt Food.
Photo courtesy of Deborah Henson-Conant

There's nothing half-baked about this eccentric collection of fire-fossilized food. Over the years Henson-Conant has cooked up, entirely by accident, the Forever Shrimp Kebab; Well, Well Done Soy Pups; and Trice-Baked Potatoes.

The entire collection is on limited public display in Henson-Conant's home by invitation only, but it can be viewed by the masses at http://burntfoodmuseum.com.

HEY, CITGO SIGN, CLAM UP!
Cambridge

L iterally and figuratively sitting in the shadow of Boston's famous Citgo sign is one owned by competitor Shell Oil, just across the Charles River. Built in 1933 and in operation continuously ever since, the giant scallop-shell neon is one of two that were constructed for Shell's regional headquarters on Commonwealth Avenue in Boston. In 1944, possibly in response to wartime restrictions, the company removed the signs. One was dismantled; the surviving spectacular neon sign was relocated to the existing Shell gas station on Memorial Drive. The Cambridge Historical Commission deemed the sign an artifact of early commercial development in the city. The Commission designated the Shell sign a historic and protected landmark, and in 1994 the sign was put on the National Register of Historic Places.

The Shell sign is at the intersection of Magazine Street and Memorial Drive, Cambridge.

*Memorial Drive in Cambridge is home
to the giant Shell Oil sign.*
Photo by Bruce Gellerman

IT'S MIT BY A SMOOT
Cambridge

The techies who attend Massachusetts Institute of Technology (MIT) deal with precise standard units of measure: the angstrom, the meter, the light year, and the smoot. The latter, while perhaps unfamiliar to lay persons, is an exacting measure: precisely 5 feet 7 inches.

There are just two things in the known universe measured in smoots: the Harvard Bridge connecting the MIT campus in Cambridge to Boston's Back Bay (364.4 smoots plus one ear) and Oliver R. Smoot Jr., MIT class of '62 (one smoot).

In October 1958, when O. R. Smoot Jr. was an MIT freshman pledge to the Lambda Chi Alpha fraternity, a fraternity brother decided it would be useful if students walking back to campus from Boston during the fog and snow knew how much further they had to walk. Smoot, the smallest of the pledges, was measured with a string, and the unit known as the smoot was born. The fraternity members marked off the smoots in paint on the bridge. When a police van appeared at about the 300-smoot mark, the measurers took off, returning later to finish the job.

Today the pledge class of Lambda Chi Alpha repaints the smoots with a new color twice a year, and the police are no longer a problem. In fact, officers use the markers to indicate locations on the bridge when writing up accident reports. To make matters easier, the Continental Construction Company of Cambridge now makes concrete sidewalk slabs 5 feet 7 inches long to coincide with the smoots, instead of the usual 6-foot increments.

Can it be too much longer before the Boston Marathon is measured in smoots, not miles?

The Harvard Bridge is measured in smoots . . .
plus one ear.
Photo by Bruce Gellerman

You can count the smoots yourself by walking over the Harvard Bridge from Massachusetts Avenue in Cambridge to Boston. (By the way, MIT named the span Harvard Bridge, even though it is located next to the MIT campus. The school considered it an example of inferior engineering and gave the dubious honor to its arch-rival down Massachusetts Avenue.)

GEORGE WASHINGTON'S PHEASANTS
UNDER GLASS
Cambridge

Harvard's Museum of Natural History is an eclectic and eccentric collection of stuffed stuff, embalmed animals, and mounted fossils. It includes a dodo, giant tape worms, a thirty-five-million-year-old bee, the world's largest frog, and the only known kronosaurus, a 42-foot-long prehistoric marine reptile. The museum is also home to the Ware Collection of Blaschka Glass Models of Plants. The unique collection of lifelike plants made out of glass was the life's work and passion of Leopold Blaschka and his son Rudolph. There are over 3,000 plants representing more than 800 species.

A pair of George Washington's pheasants reside in a glass corner case, a gift to the founding father from the Marquis de Lafayette. When the pheasants died, a taxidermist had them stuffed and mounted. The birds must have overheard a foul (or is it fowl?) mouthed visitor, because they were recently put on indefinite loan to a museum in Philadelphia.

The museum building itself, at 26 Oxford Street in Cambridge, belongs in a museum. It's a nineteenth-century throwback to the days when museums had rich wood paneling on the walls, high ceilings, and white frosted globe lights. Set aside a couple of hours to see all of the exhibits, and be sure to stop by what may be the most curious oddity in the entire museum: the antique wooden telephone booth on the second-floor staircase. It may be the last of its kind in Cambridge, if not in all of Massachusetts, and it still works.

It Makes War and Peace Look Like a Skirmish

Cambridge

I f you wanted to snuggle up for a little bedtime reading with the book *Bhutan: A Visual Odyssey Across the Last Himalayan Kingdom,* you'd better have a very big bed. Actually, the book is so big it could *be* your bed. According to the *Guinness Book of Records,* the 114-page tome is the largest commercial book ever published. It is 5 feet high, opens to

Michael Hawley, publisher and author of Bhutan—A Visual Odyssey Across the Last Himalayan Kingdom, *standing next to the world's largest published book at Acme Bookbinding where the books are made.* Photo by Paul Parisi/Courtesy of Michael Hawley

nearly 7 feet wide, and weighs more than 130 pounds. Two gallons of ink are needed to print each volume, which costs $10,000. Most of the proceeds go to charity to send students from Bhutan abroad to study.

The hefty read is the creation of Michael Hawley, director of special projects at the Massachusetts Institute of Technology. Hawley was inspired by numerous trips to the remote Shangri-La kingdom. He also wanted to demonstrate state-of-the art publishing technology.

Bhutan's leaders have charted a unique course for their country. The government's stated economic plan is to achieve the highest level of "gross national happiness." Television was not even allowed into the country until 1999, no doubt because the Bhutanese are very big readers.

The Acme Bookbinding Company in Charlestown, Massachusetts, is the exclusive builder of *Bhutan: A Visual Odyssey Across the Last Himalayan Kingdom.* Acme calls itself not only "the world's oldest book bindery," but also the world's "largest book" bindery. Acme has more information about the big book on its Web site, www.acmebook.com/index/2003/12/15.

WHO SAID GRIME DOESN'T PAY?
Cambridge

Since 1977, Elizabeth Magliozzi's sons have been driving radio listeners nuts and sending them reaching for their dials. Her boys, Tom and Ray, better known as Click and Clack of the weekly show *Car Talk* are a public-radio phenomenon. These days they have 2 million listeners a week, from Sweden to Sheboygan. The gregarious grease monkeys are a mega-industry perpetually trying to unload their books, records, T-shirts, and whatever else they can get away with on their

Car Talk Plaza, appropriately located above the Curious George shop in Harvard Square, is the intergalactic headquarters of public radio grease monkeys Click and Clack. Photo by Bruce Gellerman

shameless e-commerce Web site. The entire shenanigans come
out of *Car Talk*'s dumpy offices high above Harvard Square in
Cambridge, a.k.a. "our fair city," and can be found above the
Curious George store at the intersection of Massachusetts
Avenue and JFK Street.

Whatever you do, don't drive like these brothers.

THE THAIS THAT BIND
Cambridge

In Cambridge, at an intersection at the edge of Brattle Square
(which is actually just an intersection on the edge of Harvard
Square), you will find yet another square with a curious name.
King Bhumibol Adulyadei Square commemorates the reign of
the only monarch born on American soil. His Majesty, King Bhumibol of Thailand, was born at Mount Auburn Hospital in Cambridge in 1927 while his parents studied medicine at Harvard.

King Bhumibol ascended to the Thai throne in 1946, and in
2000 he became the longest-reigning ruler in the world. King
Bhumibol is also the only reigning monarch ever to win a gold
medal—or any medal, for that matter—at an international sporting event. He won a medal for sailing in the Southeast Asian
Peninsular Games. The King was also the first member of a
royal family ever to receive a patent. In 2003 he received his
fourth patent, for inventing an artificial rainmaking technique.

A photograph of the King can be found next to the eleva-
tors on the maternity floor at Mount Auburn hospital.

If you want to learn more about the Cambridge–Thailand
connection, ask for Joe at the Union Oyster House in Boston.
In addition to being the owner of the restaurant, Joe Milano is
Honorary Counsul of Thailand.

HARVARD UNIVERSITY'S FAMOUS
OVER-ACHIEVING NON-GRADS
Cambridge

Some of the most distinguished people in the world have earned diplomas from Harvard University, including seven U.S. Presidents, poet T. S. Eliot, authors Norman Mailer and John Updike, educator W. E. B. DuBois, jurist Oliver Wendell Holmes, Sen. Elizabeth Dole, and many more household names.

And then there is the list of equally distinguished Harvard students who walked the same hallowed halls but never graduated. Among those who dropped out of Harvard or were otherwise "excused" are actor Matt Damon; poets Robert Lowell, Robert Frost, and Ogden Nash; and Edwin Land, inventor of the Polaroid camera and holder of more than 500 patents. R. Buckminster Fuller dropped out twice—once during midterms so he could take a dancer and her entire chorus to dinner. William Randolph Hearst got the boot after sending personally inscribed chamber pots to his professors while they were considering his academic probation, and bazillionaire Bill Gates left Harvard in his junior year to devote his energies to his fledgling start-up, Microsoft.

Pop singer Bonnie Raitt never made it through. Neither did folk singer Pete Seeger, although he was honored years later with the Harvard Arts Medal, telling the crowd that he "was tempted to accept (it) on behalf of all Harvard dropouts."

THE ARCHIVE OF USELESS RESEARCH
Cambridge

At last count, there were fifty-six current or former members of the MIT community who had won a Nobel Prize. The Institute is a center for superb scholarship, intellectual excellence, innovative entrepreneurship, and some of the craziest, crackpot pseudoscientific research you will ever find in one place. In room 14N–118 of the Hayden Library's Special Collections, collection number MC 187 consists of six large boxes known as MIT's Archive of Useless Research. It's a reminder that sometimes scientific exploration respects no boundaries, even when it should.

The archive began at MIT's Engineering Library as "the American Institute of Useless Research," a collection of crank files sent to the school's researchers over the years. In 1940 Albert Ingalls, an editor for *Scientific American,* began adding useless but invaluable research that had come his way, and the Institute morphed into today's current archive. Although the archive stopped adding to the collection in 1965, it certainly was not for lack of ongoing kooky research.

The collection is a celebration of screwball science, unpublished articles, self-published books, and rejected theories sent to MIT researchers over the years and deemed deserving of preservation for posterity. Included are such breakthrough studies as "Darwin as a Pirate" and "The Riddle of the Universe *Solved.*"

The archive can be seen at the Hayden Library, 160 Memorial Drive, Cambridge. The archivist suggests you call ahead at (617) 253–5690 so they can retrieve this fascinating collection in advance of your visit.

Bring your aluminum foil helmet.

IT'S KISMET, THE ROBO SAPIEN
Cambridge

Kismet is a moody infant. One minute sad; the next happy; a few seconds later, angry; then calm, bored, or surprised. If Kismet were a baby with colic, you could understand, but Kismet isn't a baby. Kismet is a robot—more accurately, a seven-pound robot head. Still, that is enough to land Kismet in the *Guinness Book of Records* for being the most emotionally responsive robot ever built.

Kismet is the world's most expressive robot, but MIT robo-scientists did not quit while they were ahead. They have built a robot with a body, too.
Photo by Bruce Gellerman

Created by Dr. Cynthia Breazeal at the Massachusetts Institute of Technology, Kismet has movable facial features that can express basic human emotions, and electronic eyes and ears to interact with its environment and people. If you stop playing with Kismet, it acts bored; shake a doll in front of the dismembered head and it looks agitated. Kismet's gremlinlike features are powered by twenty-one motors and fifteen huge computers.

It is a good thing that Kismet has been retired to the MIT Museum, or it would have the look of envy that comes with sibling rivalry. Back in the lab, Kismet has a big brother, COG, a 7-foot-tall artificial humanoid with arms, hands, a sense of touch, and the ability to talk. To make COG even more humanlike, researchers are working on a biochemical system to run it. Ultimately, it is hoped that COG will have the intelligence equivalence of a two-year-old child.

It's the stuff of science fiction, complete with profound philosophical implications. Of course, there are also practical concerns. Perhaps robo-researchers will know they have gone too far when the machines they create in their own image start asking for the car keys.

You can see Kismet and videos of it interacting with its creator at the MIT Museum, 265 Massachusetts Avenue. For more information, check out the museum's Web site, http://web.mit .edu/museum/ or call (617) 253–4444.

MIT EAGER BEAVERS REACH FOR THE BRASS RAT
Cambridge

Graduates of the Massachusetts Institute of Technology receive a special badge of honor and symbol of intellectual distinction and achievement for studying day and night, sweat-

By tradition, the Brass Rat contains secret codes and symbols. In this design, hidden in the waves of the Charles River along the MIT campus, are the letters "A=B=C=P" representing the fact that the class of 2005 was the last to have pass/no record in their entire freshman year. Notice the hand of the student drowning in the river. The "ZZZ" to the right of the beaver's tail is for the constant attention to the student's lack of sleep. See if you can find the letters IHTFP. Photo courtesy of MIT

ing through brain-bending tests, and ruining their social lives. It's a brass rat. That's the name affectionately bestowed on MIT's class ring, which, since 1930, has featured the MIT mascot, the beaver. After all, like MIT students, beavers are nocturnal, industrious, and master builders, but on the ring, the beaver, which is an aquatic rodent, looks like a rat. Hence, the nickname.

The design changes each year, created by a committee from each class that spends the better part of a year meeting in secret. By tradition the design contains the letters *IHTFP,* an acronym with a number of interpretations underscoring the love-hate relationship MIT students have with their school. Some say it means, "I Have Truly Found Perfection." Others say it stands for "I Hate This !$@#% Place." Both camps proudly wear the brass rat; nearly 95 percent of the student body buys one.

Another tradition is the way the students wear their rings, which they purchase in their sophomore year. As undergraduates, the bottom of the beaver faces in toward the student; at the graduation ceremony, the class *en masse* removes the rings and turns them the other way. The saying is that while they are students, the beaver excretes on them, but after they graduate, it excretes on the world.

TRUTH BE TOLD, HARVARD'S STATUE IS A LIAR
Cambridge

For a university whose motto is "Veritas," you would expect the truth, the whole truth, and nothing but the truth. But check out the statue of the venerable school's namesake, John Harvard, standing right in front of University Hall. It's a pack of lies. In fact, it is informally called the Statue of Three Lies.

The inscription beneath the statue reads JOHN HARVARD, FOUNDER, 1638. Not a word of it is true.

John Harvard was not the founder of Harvard University. The college (it was a college back then) was founded in 1636 by the Massachusetts Bay Colony in what was then the village of Newtowne and later became Cambridge. John Harvard was an

The Statue of Three Lies sits in Harvard Yard.
Photo by Bruce Gellerman

early benefactor of the college and it was named for him in 1639 after he donated his library to the school. Nor is the statue a likeness of John Harvard. There were no pictures or images of him, so the sculptor, Daniel Chester French, randomly chose a student as his model and dressed him in seventeenth-century garb.

And, truth be told, the statue actually contains *four*, not three, lies. The statue is *not* of John Harvard, who was *not* the founder of Harvard University, which was *not* founded in 1638, and does *not* stand in Harvard Yard in front of University Hall. It sits.

WHAT YOU GET WHEN YOU CROSS EINSTEIN WITH THE THREE STOOGES

Cambridge

You have to hand it to those techno-nerds at MIT: They sure know how to hack. Since the technical institute first opened in 1861, the brainy students have been pulling creative practical jokes that are both technically challenging and devilishly clever. Over the years the ever-more-ambitious hacks, as they are called, have become an institution.

Some pranks have been elegantly simple, like the stoplight altered to read "don't walk–chew," instead of "walk." Others were more scientifically challenging. In 1976, for example, hackers consulted an arachnologist and used an electron microscope to study spider webs before weaving a wicked-big one out of 1,250 feet of wire and rope and installing it in a campus building. The real trick, as with all hacks, was not to get snared by the police.

In 1982, during the Harvard–Yale football game, hackers hid a weather balloon inscribed with "MIT" under the turf of Harvard's 40-yard line. The pranksters inflated the balloon by remote control. The crowd and teams looked aghast as the balloon grew to 6 feet in diameter and exploded in a burst of white smoke. MIT one, Harvard–Yale zero.

MIT's famed domes have long been favorite places for hackers to pull their pranks. One Halloween, hackers dressed the Great Dome in a 20-foot-tall witch's hat. Another year the huge dome was transformed into the Star Wars robot R2D2. The dome has been topped with a working telephone booth that rang when officials tried to remove it. Hackers also turned the pinnacle into a parking space for a full-size replica of a campus police car, complete with working lights, with a box of dough-nuts on the front seat.

The 1982 weather balloon inflator that disrupted
the Harvard–Yale football game.
Photo by Bruce Gellerman

Hacks have to be harmless as well as humorous. Self-deprecating humor works well. In 1996 MIT student hackers transformed the Great Dome into a giant, working propeller beanie. Who says nerds have no sense of humor?

A P L A C E T O B E C A U G H T D E A D I N
C a m b r i d g e

T here are almost as many people buried in Mount Auburn Cemetery in Cambridge (93,000 and counting) as there are living in the city (101,000). The historic cemetery is a popular place for very permanent residents and visitors alike. More than 200,000 people a year visit the burial grounds, making it one of Cambridge's most popular tourist destinations.

Founded in 1831 by the Massachusetts Horticultural Society, Mount Auburn was the first landscaped cemetery in America. Its creation marked a dramatic change in the prevailing attitudes about death and burial, as it was designed not only to be a decent place of interment but also to serve as a cultural institution. Mount Auburn, unlike other early city cemeteries, utilized landscape architecture in its planning. This influenced the creation of no less than fifteen other park–cemeteries in the United States. Besides its obvious function, Mount Auburn also serves as a museum, a sculpture garden, an arboretum, and a wildlife sanctuary.

Among the notables making the 175-acre garden their final residence are Oliver Wendell Holmes, Winslow Homer, Fanny Farmer, B. F. Skinner, and Buckminster Fuller.

The gravesite of Mary Baker Eddy, founder of the Church of Christ, Scientist, is one of the more spectacular. And contrary to long-standing rumors, she did not have a telephone installed in her crypt. During the construction of her monument, Eddy's body was kept in the cemetery's receiving vault. A guard was hired to stay with the body until it was interred and the tomb was sealed. A telephone was installed at the receiving vault for the guard's use during that period. There was never a phone at Eddy's monument.

Mount Auburn Cemetery is open every day of the year from 8:00 A.M. to 5:00 P.M. During daylight saving time hours are extended to 7:00 P.M. Drive-by and walking audio tours are available on tape for rent or purchase at the entrance gate or the office. The cemetery is located at 580 Mount Auburn Street, Cambridge. For additional information, call (617) 547–7105.

HEARD ON THE GRAPEVINE: SOMETIMES YOU DON'T REAP WHAT YOU SOW
Concord

Ephraim Wales Bull is buried in Concord's Sleepy Hollow Cemetery alongside some very distinguished company. Here, along Authors Ridge, you will find the gravesites of Henry Thoreau (1862), Nathaniel Hawthorne (1864), Ralph Waldo Emerson (1882), and Louisa May Alcott (1888) and her father, Bronson Alcott (1888). Okay; admittedly, Ephraim Wales Bull's name is not as familiar as these literary greats, but his contribution to the nation looms just as large. You see, Ephraim Wales Bull is the "father of the Concord grape." Today U.S. grape farmers harvest more Concord grapes than all other varieties combined.

Now, by all rights you should not even be able to grow grapes in Massachusetts. The grape killing frost comes early in fall and lasts until late spring. Nevertheless, Bull was, well, bullheaded. He persevered for ten years to develop his plump, purple berry, testing thousand of seedlings on his Concord farm before he came across his hardy, all-American variety.

Bull sold cuttings from his divine vine for $1,000 each, yet despite the horticultural breakthrough he died a poor man. His gravestone is inscribed, "He sowed—others reaped."

Among those who reaped was Vineland, New Jersey, dentist Thomas Welch, who began squeezing Bull's grapes with vigor in 1869. His company, Welch's, began producing unfermented sacramental wine. In 1913 Secretary of the State William Jennings Bryan served Welch's Grape Juice instead of wine at a state dinner for the outgoing British ambassador. The uproar in the press resulted in months of free publicity.

Ephraim Wales Bull's farmhouse, Grapevine Cottage, still stands on Lexington Road. The original vine from which all of the world's Concord grapes are descendants can still be seen.

An interesting note: A Massachusetts law regulates the taking of photographs and movies in a public cemetery for commercial purposes. To receive permission to do so, contact the cemetery department at (978) 318–3233.

Sleepy Hollow Cemetery is on Bedford Street just off the rotary in the center of Concord.

ART TOO BAD TO BE IGNORED
Dedham

The Museum of Bad Art (MOBA) is testimony to the wisdom of writer Marshall McLuhan, who said, "Art is anything you can get away with." The museum is dedicated to "the collection, preservation, exhibition, and celebration of bad art in all its forms and all its glory." In short, it's a permanent repository for art too bad to be ignored.

What started out in 1995 in a suburban basement as a humble assemblage of spectacularly awful artwork has evolved into a full-fledged museum, complete with the requisite gift shop. The MOBA holds a special place near and dear to connoisseurs

Sunday on the Pot with George *sits in the Museum of Bad Art.* Photo © Museum of Bad Art, Dedham, Massachusetts

of misunderstood masterpieces. It's also located within earshot of the men's room at the Dedham Community Theater.

To qualify for an esteemed place in the museum's collection, an artist's ambition has to vastly exceed his or her ability. One classic museum piece, for example, portrays a naked woman in stiletto heels and red leg warmers sitting on a stool milking a unicorn. The unicorn looks startled but not displeased by the experience. It's truly a head-snapping, jaw-dropping sight.

MOBA curators are constantly searching Salvation Army stores and landfills in search of the highest caliber bad art. The majority of the collection came from bequests of the public refuse system. Submissions are always welcome. The curators have imposed a $6.50 limit on acquiring new works but once offered twice that amount as a reward for a piece that was stolen. (Alas, even at that price the painting was never recovered.)

MOBA's permanent gallery is at the Dedham Community Theater, 580 High Street in Dedham Center. For more information visit www.glyphs.com/moba.

THE MAN WHO INVENTED MONEY
Lexington

Charles Ponzi was a small man with a taste for the finer things in life. He loved luxurious houses and large automobiles, and he dressed in the finest top hats, walking sticks, and suits. Too bad he couldn't afford them. No matter; the former dishwasher, convicted smuggler, and scam artist was "the man who invented money." At the peak of his pyramid scheme in 1919, Ponzi was raking in a million dollars a week. He created 40,000 "millionaires" and at one point sauntered into the Hanover Trust Company, opened a suitcase with $3 million in cash, and bought a controlling interest in the bank.

The pyramid scam is probably as old as, well, the pyramids. But it took Charles Ponzi, an Italian immigrant living in Boston, to raise it to new heights in the world of modern finance. The scam is simple: Borrow from Peter to pay back money you borrowed from Paul. Repeat over and over again and, voila: You have a Ponzi scheme. A bit like Social Security, the system works as long as you bring in enough new investors at the bottom to support those at the top of the pyramid.

Ponzi employed a new twist on the old scam. He promised investors a 50 percent return on their money in ninety days if they purchased international postal reply coupons, which were coupons he bought overseas for a penny and exchanged in the United States for six cents. (Unfortunately, it wound up costing more money to ship and exchange the coupons than they were worth here, but that was a minor detail to Ponzi.)

Ponzi's house of reply coupons finally collapsed when a Boston newspaper questioned the con. Ultimately, five banks went belly-up in the scam. Ponzi wound up spending seven years in a Boston jail and died penniless in Rio de Janeiro. He left behind an unfinished manuscript for a book, appropriately titled *The Fall of Mr. Ponzi.*

As Ponzi's wife, Sophie, watched, investigators searched their twenty-room mansion in Lexington, Massachusetts, for securities and evidence of fraud. All they found were one hundred gallons of homemade Italian wine.

The stucco house in Lexington still stands. It's the third on the right on Slocumb Street, off Massachusetts Avenue.

BLACK DAHLIA MONUMENT
Medford

One of the stranger monuments in Massachusetts was designed and paid for by documentary filmmaker Kyle J. Wood, whose film *Medford Girl* chronicles the life and death of Elizabeth Short, "the Black Dahlia." Short was born in Hyde Park, Massachusetts, in 1924 and grew up in Medford. She quit school at age sixteen, seeking fame and fortune in Hollywood. Her mutilated body, severed in half at the waist, was found in a vacant lot in Hollywood in 1947—one of the most celebrated unsolved mysteries of its time.

The Black Dahlia monument is located at 115 Salem Street in Medford.

JUMBO IN A JAR
Medford

Although students at Tufts University are called Jumbos, it's not that they are especially big. They hold that nickname because the school's original mascot was P. T. Barnum's famous elephant, Jumbo. Born in Africa in 1859, Jumbo grew to 12 feet high at the shoulder and weighed more than six tons. Barnum, ever the showman, billed the huge pachyderm as the largest land animal ever in captivity. Big as he was, today all that remains of Jumbo are some ashes stored in a fourteen-ounce Peter Pan peanut butter jar locked in the safe of the school's athletic director.

The story of how Jumbo went from circus center ring to a crunchy peanut butter jar at college begins in 1882, when Barnum bought Jumbo from the London Zoo for $10,000. Jumbo traveled the circus circuit in a specially built railroad car until 1885, when he was hit by a train and died. The pachyderm underwent taxidermy and the stuffed hide was taken on a four-year world tour. Jumbo then came to his final resting place at the Barnum Museum at Tufts University, where the ringmaster was a school trustee. He stood there for eighty-six years, while generations of students stuffed his trunk with pennies and pulled his tail for good luck on tests. In 1942 Jumbo underwent an overhaul and his original over-tugged tail was archived at the school's library.

All was well until 1975, when a fire destroyed the Barnum building, rendering everything, including the elephant, into a pile of ashes. Mindful of the mascot's importance to Tufts, a member of the school's athletic department scooped up what he assumed were Jumbo's ashes and put them into the container

*A jar of crunchy Peter Pan Peanut Butter is the
final resting place of Jumbo the Elephant.*
Photo by Bruce Gellerman

he had on hand—an empty peanut butter jar—which is now
kept in a safe in the athletic director's office. To this day Tufts
Jumbos rub the jar for luck just before a big game.

The tail on Jumbo's tush is in Tufts' Tisch Library Digital
Collections and Archives. Say that three times fast and win a
Kewpie doll.

ELEPHANT MAN HAS A HERD INSTINCT
Medford

It's probably a good thing that John Baronian did not attend the University of California–Santa Cruz or Cal State–Long Beach. Otherwise, you might be reading about the world's largest collection of banana slugs or dirtbags. Baronian, you see, collected miniature models of his alma mater's mascot. As luck would have it, he went to Tufts University, home of Jumbo, the elephant, and so for fifty years Baronian collected elephant figurines.

Baronian began gathering his mini-menagerie of mini *objets d'pachyderm* soon after graduation. Today he has more than 3,000 figurines in his collection—probably the largest assemblage of pachyderm art on the planet. (If you've heard of a bigger herd, let him know.) He has elephants made out of wood, glass, bronze, porcelain, and yes, ivory. He even has an elephant crafted out of camel hide. There are elephant ashtrays, mugs, jewelry, and bookends and a pachyderm jigsaw puzzle.

Baronian is not just any Jumbo alum, he's *the* jumbo Jumbo supporter. On campus he is known as "Mr. Tufts" for his long volunteer service and generosity to the University. A man with a big heart and a herd to match, he ran out of space for the collection in his home, so he donated it to the school. It now resides in the Remis Sculpture Court at the Aidekman Arts Center, 40R Talbot Avenue on Tufts' Medford campus. Call ahead for hours at (617) 627–3518.

"Mr. Tufts," John *Baronian, with members of his*
mini-elephant menagerie.
Photo by Bruce Gellerman

THE CHRISTMAS
LIGHTS FANTASTIC

Residents living on Greystone Court in
Medford (locals pronounce it "Meffuhd") go
to extreme measures to make sure all their
Christmases are bright. When the owners of the
thirteen houses on this cul-de-sac throw the
switches on their illuminated santas, reindeers,
and other lighted lawn tchotchkes, you need to
stand back. It is truly something to behold. Tens
of thousands of lights erupt in a dazzling display of December decorating. What makes the
display so remarkable is that the tradition is
unorganized. Surprisingly, there are no meetings, leaders, or plans for the show. It's an
unspoken tradition going back to the early 1990s
that neighbors here will try to out-illuminate
each other during the holiday season.

Word has spread and thousands of spectators in cars and by the busloads cruise the
street each night—a far cry from 1659, when
Massachusetts fined people for celebrating on
December 25. (It seems the Pilgrims had a dis-
trust of Christmas. Thankfully for folks in
Medford, the law was repealed in 1681.) The
electricity bills are enough of a fine for anyone.

THIS SIGN WILL SLEIGH YOU
Medford

We hate dashing your Christmas spirit, but one of the most popular songs sung around the holiday has nothing to do with Christmas. "Jingle Bells" was written by Medford resident James Pierpont in 1850, inspired by the annual one-horse open-sleigh races on Salem and Pleasant Streets between Medford Square and Malden Square. Pierpont penned the racy little ditty in Simpson's Tavern, a boardinghouse that had the only piano in town. The lyrics tell the story of picking up girls while hot-rodding through the snow.

The song was originally titled "One-Horse Open Sleigh," and initially it was a flop. But after a Boston publishing house released it as "Jingle Bells" in 1859, the rest was history, albeit controversial history. It seems that Savannah, Georgia, thinks it's the "Jingle Bells capital of the world" because Pierpont was living there when the song was released and is also buried there. However, a plaque at 21 High Street near the corner of Forest Street in Medford sets things right. As residents in Medford are quick to point out, Pierpont wrote the tune while in Massachusetts . . . and racing a sleigh in snowless Savannah doesn't make much sense, anyway. (In fairness to Savannah, it too has a plaque commemorating the composer of "Jingle Bells.")

Medford is also where the lyrics for another famous festive song were written. Town resident Lydia Maria Child's poem "Boy's Thanksgiving" became the song "Over the River and Through the Woods." Child lived in the Greek Revival house at 114 Ashland Street on the corner of Salem Street, not far from where Pierpont sleighed them with "Jingle Bells." Behind Child's house are the woods she went through and the Mystic River over which she traveled to get to Grandfather's house. We're told the horse knows the way.

THE COCKROACHES THAT
ALMOST ATE NATICK
Natick

On the battlefield of the future, it may be the suit that makes the soldier. The uniforms warriors will wear decades from now are being designed at the U.S. Army Soldier Systems Center in Natick, about 20 miles due west of Boston.

The Center is a high-tech laboratory that designs and develops everything a soldier wears, carries, or consumes. Established in 1954, the lab created the technology that led to freeze-dried food. During the Vietnam War it created a boot sole in the shape of a bare-footed VietCong soldier to confuse the enemy, and it designed a camouflage Jewish prayer shawl.

The Natick lab is best known for developing the field combat rations called *MREs*, or Meals Ready to Eat. The MRE menus provide high-calorie, relatively palatable foods with a shelf life that rivals enriched uranium.

In 1974 Army scientists were experimenting with a new way to control pests by zapping them with ultraviolet rays. Unfortunately, the experiment went out of control. The zapped bugs were put in plastic bags with a chemical, then disposed of at a local dump. The chemical ate through the bags and the bugs' eggs hatched and escaped into Natick. The insects, 4-inch flying Madagascar cockroaches, drove residents buggy. The cockroaches were resistant to most pesticides and the Army had to call in the "big guns" and use DDT.

Researchers at the Natick facility are now working on projects designed to protect our men and women in uniform with fabrics that change color depending on their surrounding environment, and spray-on clothing.

Due to budget cuts and the cost of fighting current wars, the Soldier Systems Center is not conducting tours for the public. However, its Web site, www.natick.army.mil, provides a good overview of the ongoing research. The bugs won't get out as easy that way, either.

NEWTON'S CONTRIBUTION TO COOKIEDOM
Newton

I n 1891 James Henry Mitchell invented a contraption that could squish figs into jam and smear the substance between two layers of soft, crumbly cookie dough. The cookies were a smash hit, and soon the Kennedy Biscuit Works in Cambridge was turning them out by the truck load.

The Big Fig, as usual, is right in the middle of things.
Photo courtesy of Newton History Museum at the Jackson
Homestead, Newton, Massachusetts

The famous cookie got its name from the plant manager at the bakery, who liked to name his cookies and crackers after surrounding Massachusetts towns. Thankfully he didn't decide to dub his latest concoction after Cow Yard, Massachusetts, or Marblehead, and instead settled on the suburban city of Newton.

An apartment building now stands at 129 Franklin Street on the site near MIT where the original factory baked Fig Newtons by the billions. Several of the original biscuit ovens have been preserved there, and above the front door is a giant rendition of the cookie itself.

Nabisco Brands eventually bought the Kennedy Biscuit Works, and to commemorate the one-hundredth anniversary of the Fig Newton, it threw a bash for the cookies' namesake community. The Big Fig acted like the fruit he is and, of course, was right in the center of things.

B E A U T I F U L   B L A B B E R M O U T H   B R I D G E
N e w t o n

Echo Bridge is one of the highest stone arches in the world—its crown is 51 feet above the Charles River—but what makes it truly remarkable is that, as the name implies, the bridge talks back to you, and back to you, and back to you.

Built in 1876 to carry water to Boston, the 500-foot-long aqueduct consists of seven arches. The largest segment, spanning the Charles, is 130 feet long, and it is this arch that produces the remarkable reverberation. It's said that on a still day the granite walls can bounce a human voice back and forth as many as eighteen times. (Be forewarned: You might not always like the responses you get. Try yelling the word *July* under the archway.)

For a spectacular view of the Charles River, stand atop the bridge's pedestrian promenade. The span is located at the end of Chestnut Street, north of Route 9 in the Upper Charles River Reservation. It is open from dawn to dusk year-round.

MARATHON MAN
Newton

John Kelley likes to run and run and run. Between 1928 and 1992, John "the Elder" Kelley, a Massachusetts native, ran the Boston Marathon sixty-one times, finishing all but three races. He came in first in two races (1935 and 1945), took second place a record seven times, and finished in the top ten eighteen times.

At the foot of Heart Break Hill is the monument
to Boston Marathon man John Kelley.
Photo by Bruce Gellerman

Kelley ran his last marathon when he was eighty-five and became the first road runner elected to the National Track and Field Hall of Fame. Officials waived the retirement rule because they figured he might never retire.

A statue dedicated to the amazing marathoner as a young man and as an older participant is located at Heart Break Hill, on the corner of Walnut Street and Commonwealth Avenue in Newton, across from City Hall.

In the 1996 centennial running of the Boston Marathon, 39,708 official entrants participated in the race. According to the *Guinness Book of Records,* this is the largest number of runners in a single race in history.

MAYBE IT WAS SO THE WORMS DIDN'T HAVE TO USE THE STAIRS?
Newton

I t's called simply the Old Stone Barn, but don't let the plain name deceive you. This is one strange structure. Built in 1839, the huge stone building (100 feet by 50 feet) has an architectural feature you don't see every day: All four stories have access to ground level. The architectural feat was accomplished by building the barn into dirt embankments. The sub-basement faces the east; the basement, the south; the first floor, the west; and the second floor, the north, off Cliff Road.

Historians are not sure why the barn was built this way, or even if it was originally intended to be a barn. The owner, Otis Pette Sr., never told anyone why he had it constructed. After it was built it lay empty for years until it was used as a stable. Some speculate that Pette meant for the barn to house a silk-

The Old Stone Barn has access to ground level from all four stories.
Photo courtesy of Newton History Museum at the Jackson Homestead,
Newton, Massachusetts

worm hatchery and constructed it out of stone because his textile factory had burned to the ground earlier that year. However, the silkworm industry quickly unraveled in colonial New England. (The cold killed the mulberry bushes.)

The Old Stone Barn, or whatever it was, still stands and is used as a warehouse. It can be seen at 38–44 Oak Street, off Cliff Road in Newton Upper Falls.

THE ORIGINAL AIRHEAD AND HIS IGNOBLE IG NOBEL PRIZES
Somerville

Marc Abrahams is an airhead and proud of it. In fact, as publisher of the *Annals of Improbable Research,* or *AIR,* Abrahams is head airhead. *AIR* is what would happen if the editors of *Mad* magazine and the *National Lampoon* conspired to publish *Scientific American.* And lest you think being an airhead is somehow an ignoble distinction, the magazine has eight Nobel Prize laureates on its editorial board.

Since 1990 *AIR* has injected spoofs, parodies, and satires into the otherwise straightlaced world of science and scientists. Example of typical articles include: "Why the Chicken Must Come First," "Mass Strandings of Horseshoe Crabs," and an inquiry titled "What Does Crime Taste Like?" A regular feature queries Nobel Prize winners with the most pressing questions of our time, such as, "Do you shave with a blade razor or electric?" and "Do you often give people nicknames?"

The highlight of the year for Abrahams and *AIR* is the annual Ig Nobel Prize ceremony, honoring people whose achievements "cannot or should not be reproduced." This take-off on the Stockholm proceedings includes some of the pomp along with a heavy dose of Swedish slapstick. Abrahams sports a tuxedo and top hat to announce the winners, including a biologist who studied how various flavors of chewing gum affect brain waves. Karl Kruszelnicki of the University of Sydney received his Ig Nobel Prize for his comprehensive survey of human belly button lint: who gets it, when, what color, and how much. Chris McManus of University College, London was honored for his excruciatingly balanced report, "Scrotal Asymmetry in Man and in Ancient Sculpture." Anders Barheim and

Hogne Sandvik received their Ig Nobel Biology Prize in 1996 for their monumental discovery that sour cream stimulates the appetite of leeches. Jerald Bain and Kerry Siminoski won the Ig in Statistics in 1998 for their landmark study, "The Relationship among Height, Penile Length, and Foot Size."

The Ig ceremony, featuring opera, interpretive dance by Nobel laureates, and drama takes place in Sanders Theater at Harvard University the first week of October, and is broadcast on National Public Radio's *Science Friday,* the day after Thanksgiving. Check your local listings and be prepared to fall out of your seat.

ANY SEAT IN A STORM

New England Nor'easter snowstorms are legendary for their ferocity. So are folks from Somerville, Massachusetts. After residents shovel out their parking spaces along the city's narrow streets, they jealously guard their clearings by putting lawn chairs, chaise longues, even sofas in the street to hold "their" spots. It's not unusual to see bundled-up Somervillians sitting on their furniture, waiting for the family car to return.

Saving shoveled-out spots in the snow is a time-honored winter tradition in Somerville, and heaven help those who violate the unwritten rules of the road. If you do, make sure you have towing insurance and are prepared to buy four new tires.

ONE ARTIST YOU DEFINITELY DON'T WANT TO PAINT YOUR PORTRAIT
Watertown

Part of the permanent collection at the Armenian Library and Museum of America in Watertown, Massachusetts, are pictures painted by Dr. Jack Kevorkian. Known to many as "Doctor Death," Kevorkian is a controversial physician who promotes assisted suicide and has been jailed for practicing what he preaches. Kevorkian is also an oil painter of some note, and being an ethnic Armenian, he has donated a number of his works to the Armenian Library and Museum. Two of his oils, *Very Still Life* and *Genocide,* are hanging in the museum at 65 Main Street, Watertown. For more information, call (617) 926-2562.

Dr. Jack Kevorkian's Very Still Life hangs in the Armenian Library and Museum in Watertown. Photo by Bruce Gellerman

AS THE WORLD DOESN'T TURN
Wellesley

O ne of the largest worlds in the world can be found on the campus of Babson College in Wellesley. The giant Babson Globe was built in 1955. It weighs 21.5 tons and is 38 feet in diameter. It is literally meant to provide an out-of-this-world experience, to give you an idea of what Mother Earth would look like if you stood 5,000 miles away in space. Each inch on

The 21.5-ton globe at Babson College stopped
revolving in 1993.
Photo by Bruce Gellerman

the steel ball represents 24 miles. The globe rotated on its base and spun on its axis until sometime in 1993, when the mechanical turning-and-spinning device broke. The earth has stood still ever since.

Truth be told, there are larger globes. The Unisphere, from the 1964 New York World's Fair in Queens, is 120 feet in diameter. The world's current world record holder, Eartha, installed at the DeLorme Map company in Yarmouth, Maine, is about 41 feet in diameter.

To get up close and personal with the Babson Globe, the one-time largest world in the world, go to Babson College in Wellesley sometime during daylight hours. It's that giant round thing fixed in space outside the Coleman Map Building. There is no admission charge. Who says nothing in the world is free?

UNDERSTANDING THE GRAVITY OF THE SITUATION
Wellesley

It was Roger Babson's dream that what went up would not necessarily have to come down. To accomplish this gravity-defying feat, Babson created the Gravity Research Foundation in 1948. Its goal was to investigate ways to block and harness the force of gravity.

The idea of violating a basic law of physics may sound far out, but Babson was a man who had his feet firmly on the ground. A self-made millionaire who earned his money revolutionizing the financial services industry, Babson also founded two universities, ran for president of the United States against FDR (he came in third out of eight candidates), and authored forty-seven books.

In one of his books, *Gravity—Our Enemy No. 1* Babson explained his quest to tame the pull of the earth. It was a personal battle, as he blamed gravity for his son's death in an airplane crash and for his sister's drowning, writing of the latter, "She was unable to fight gravity, which came up and seized her like a dragon and brought her to the bottom."

The Gravity Research Foundation, which recently relocated to Babson College in Wellesley, holds an annual convention and essay contest. Although the contest does attract its share of crackpots, it also receives submissions from some of the best minds of our time. Famed cosmologist Stephen Hawking has won the foundation's cash prize five times.

The foundation has also installed a number of granite monuments on college campuses where distinguished anti-gravity research was being done. One monument was installed in 1961 on the Tufts University campus in Somerville, Massachusetts, where it soon became a source of myth and mirth. The inscription reads: THIS MONUMENT HAS BEEN ERECTED BY THE GRAVITY RESEARCH FOUNDATION. IT IS TO REMIND STUDENTS OF THE BLESSINGS FORTHCOMING WHEN A SEMI-INSULATOR IS DISCOVERED IN ORDER TO HARNESS GRAVITY AS A FREE POWER AND REDUCE AIRPLANE ACCIDENTS.

A year after the monument's installation, a group of students dug a hole around the stone to test whether it would defy gravity. (It didn't.) Another group dug it up again and moved it to a different location. Thus began a cycle of burying and digging up that lasted several years. In 1968 Tufts groundskeepers dug up the stone to make way for a sidewalk and buried it in a secret locale. It remained hidden until 1971, when members of the Mountain Club unearthed it by sheer accident. In 1975 it was moved again. Then in 1977 the administration confiscated the stone and moved it to an undisclosed location after students had used it to block the doors of (P. T.) Barnum Hall. In the 1980s the stone was finally set to rest in its present location between Eaton Hall and Goddard Chapel.

THE MASSACHUSETTS VIKINGS

*T*hree public monuments in eastern Massachusetts
lay claim that it was Viking Leif Erikson in 1000,
not Christopher Columbus in 1492, who was the first
European to step foot on North America. The monuments were built by Eben Norton Horsford, a Harvard
professor of chemistry turned amateur archaeologist
who was convinced that "Leif the Lucky" was the first
European in the New World.

Professor Horsford made a fortune in the mid-
nineteenth century selling "Horsford's Cream of Tartar
Substitute," a new-formula baking powder, and used
the money to fund excavations in Cambridge, Weston,
and Watertown. According to Horsford, Erikson landed
on Cape Cod, sailed up the Charles River, and built a
house in what is now Cambridge. Horsford said he
found some buried Norse artifacts near the intersection
of Memorial Drive, Mount Auburn Street, and Gerry's
Landing Road. He built a small monument there marking the spot.

Further upstream stands Norumbega Tower. Horsford built the structure in 1889 to commemorate the
site on which he believed the Vikings had constructed the
legendary Norse settlement of the same name. A sum-
mary of Horsford's theory is engraved on a plaque on
the tower. To see it, take Route 128 to Route 30 West to
River Road North.

The third monument to Horsford's fanciful theory is
located at Charlesgate East on Commonwealth Avenue,
near Kenmore Square in Boston. It was unveiled in
1887 and depicts Leif the Lucky on a pedestal scanning
the distant horizon. The back of the memorial is
inscribed: LEIF THE DISCOVERER SON OF ERIK WHO SAILED
FROM ICELAND AND LANDED ON THIS CONTINENT AD 1000.

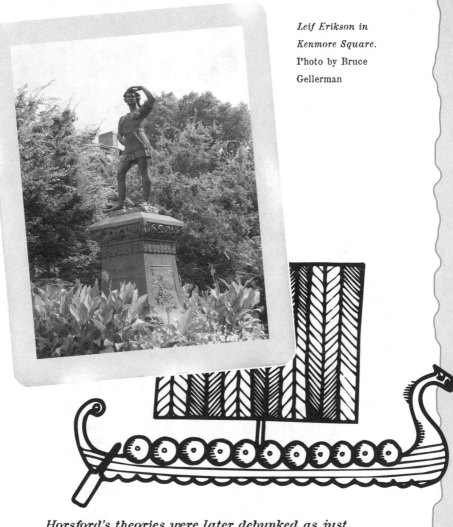

Leif Erikson in Kenmore Square. Photo by Bruce Gellerman

Horsford's theories were later debunked as just bunk, and he's considered a crackpot today. But recent scientific analysis of a controversial parchment drawing, the so-called Vinland Map, and an accompanying manuscript called "The Tartar Relation" seem to suggest that maybe the chemist was onto something archaeological after all.

A CHIP OFF THE OLD BLOCK
Wellesley

T he story about how Sir Isaac Newton got clunked on the noggin and discovered gravity isn't as far-fetched as it may sound. On the campus of Babson College stands a fifth-generation apple tree grown from a cutting of a tree from young Isaac's home in Woolsthorpe Manor, Lincolnshire, England. You'll find the area around the fenced-in tree littered with apples, proving Sir Isaac correct.

Babson College founder Charles Babson was fascinated with gravity and Newton. In addition to the Newton apple tree now growing in the center of campus, Babson also purchased the fore-parlor from the great mathematician's last London residence. He had the room disassembled and rebuilt in the Babson College library.

A chip off Newton's block grows on the
campus of Babson College.
Photo by Bruce Gellerman

NORTHEAST MASSACHUSETTS

NORTHEAST
MASSACHUSETTS

THERE'S DEFINITELY SOMETHING UP HIS SLEEVE
Beverly

It seems the only thing magician Cesareo Palaez can't make disappear is his magic show. In 1972 Palaez conjured up "Le Grand David and his Own Spectacular Magic Show" out of thin air, little money, and a bunch of volunteers. Today the act is the longest-running stage magic show in the world.

The magic is not limited to the stage. It begins as soon as you enter the theater. Palaez and his troupe perform Le Grand David in two vaudeville theaters that they have meticulously restored to their former gilded glory. In the lobby, members of the troupe, many who have been with Palaez since the very beginning (and, in some cases, their children and even grand-children) entertain patrons before the stage performance starts. It's multigenerational, multitasking magic. The sets are magnificent, the costumes opulent. Members of the cast make both.

Taking center stage, of course, is Palaez, who says it's his passion for "wonder, mystery, and enchantment" that brings so many people under his spell. A professor emeritus of psychology, Palaez is also a past president of the Society of American Magicians and was voted Magician of the Year several times. He came to the United States from Cuba, hoping to re-create the magic shows he had watched as a boy. He left his home just after Castro took power, in what he calls his greatest escape.

Palaez, starring as Marco the Magi, performs on select Thursdays at 7:30 P.M. at the Larcom Theater, 13 Wallis Street, and Sundays at 3:00 P.M. at the Cabot Street Theater, 286 Cabot Street. For more information, call (978) 927–3677. Every performance is another record-breaker.

Aw, Shucks, I Do
Essex

The fried clam is the claim to fame at the restaurant Woodman's of Essex. It was here on Main Street, along a marshy road, that Lawrence and Bessie Woodman say they invented the world's first munchy mollusk. Although others make the crunchy clam claim, they don't have the evidence the Woodmans have. Right on the back of their marriage certificate, it says they dunked the first mollusk into a deep-fryer on July 3, 1916. They said "I do," and they did. If anyone claims otherwise, let them come forward or just clam up.

The idea certainly wasn't half-baked. Come during the summer and expect a line out the door. Woodman's of Essex is on Route 133, Main Street. For more information, phone (978) 768–6057 or (800) 649–1773 or visit www.woodmans.com. (Or is it "dot-clam?")

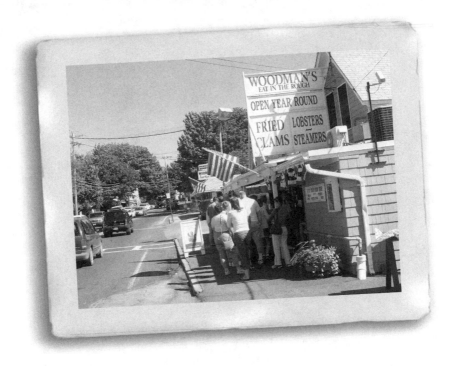

A deep fryer and clams are a marriage made in heaven at Woodman's.

Photo by Bruce Gellerman

HUNTING FOR BABSON'S BIG BOULDERS
Gloucester

By 1830, Dogtown, Massachusetts, had literally gone to the dogs. First the men left, then the women, leaving behind their canine companions. The abandoned, unincorporated town was purchased by philanthropist Charles Babson, founder of

Words to the wise can be found in Dogtown.
Photo courtesy of Don Noll © 2004 (www.don.noll.com)

Babson College. Babson hired Swedish stone carvers to chisel words to the wise into huge glacial boulders that littered the property. And today Dogtown is best known for the big boulders bearing their messages. The messages include: "Never Try, Never Win," "Be on Time," "Help Mother," and our favorite, "Get a Job."

Dogtown is now part of Gloucester and has become a favorite haunt for trail-riding bicyclists. You may have to hunt a bit to find the place. (Don't forget to take insect repellant with you.) Take Route 127 just outside of Gloucester to Reynard Street. At the end of Reynard, turn left onto Cherry Street. You'll see a small sign for Dogtown Commons. Hey, never try, never win.

A GREASY POLE AND A TOUGH ITALIAN
Gloucester

*S*ince 1931, Gloucester's Italian-American fishing community has paid homage to the patron saint of fishing by holding its annual Saint Peter's Fiesta. Here, commercial fishing is a way of life and, too often, death. Gloucester was the hailing port of the *Andrea Gail*, which encountered the Perfect Storm.

Each year contestants squirm along this greased
pole to capture a red flag.
Photo by Bruce Gellerman

According to Alphonse Millefoglie, vice president of the Fiesta Committee, the celebration's most unusual event is the Greasy Pole Contest. A heavily greased, 45-foot telephone pole is extended over the water, 200 feet off Pavillion Beach. Contestants must wiggle and squirm their way along the pole and capture a red flag nailed to the end. The winner then swims back to the beach. All the other contestants lift the victorious pole walker onto their shoulders and parade around the town.

The first round is traditionally a trial run without capturing the flag. In 1979 one contestant broke the courtesy rule and was quickly confronted by a contest enforcer, Anthony "Matza" Giambanco. Matza presented the offender with a knuckle sandwich, the flag was once again nailed to the pole, and the competition commenced.

The Fiesta is a five-day event held on the June weekend closest to the Feast of Saint Peter. It's a time for prayers, food, a parade, food, sporting events, and food . . . sometimes a knuckle sandwich. For more information, visit www.stpeters fiesta.org.

The greasy pole is a permanent fixture and can be seen year-round. It's off shore, in the harbor right behind the Cape Ann Chamber of Commerce on Commercial Street.

THE INVENTIVE GENIUS WITH AN ITCH FOR DISCOVERY
Gloucester

Couch potatoes everywhere owe a debt of gratitude to their patron saint, John Hays Hammond Jr. This inventive genius was one of the early pioneers of radio electronics and is considered "the Father of the Remote Control." Dr. Hammond patented more than 430 inventions, second in number only to

*A knight in shining armor and a pipe organ reside at the
eclectic castle built by inventor John Jay Hammond Jr.*
Photo by Bruce Gellerman

Thomas Edison. Hammond's inventions reflect his wide interests, whimsical sense of humor, and taste for the flamboyant.
In 1914 the good doctor spooked sailors and spectators when
he guided a crewless "ghost ship" by remote control on a 130-
mile round-trip cruise from his home in Gloucester Harbor to
Boston. Among his other inventions was a hypodermic meat
baster, a stove that cooks food without using a pan, and a mag-
netic bottle cap remover. Alas, his cure for baldness failed, suc-
ceeding only in turning his scalp green.

Most of Hammond's creations had military applications. During World War II he offered the United States and Great Britain his patent to a fire bomb. Although the Allies turned him down, Hammond was arrested for treason when Germany subsequently used it on England. He was freed only after one of his staff members admitted to selling the weapon to the enemy.

Hammond did much of his inventing in a medieval-style castle he constructed in Gloucester from 1926 to 1929. In the Great Hall Hammond designed and built the largest pipe organ in a private residence in the world. It has more than 10,000 pipes. (No he's not *that* Hammond.)

When Dr. Hammond died in 1965, he was buried with his mummified cats, who tour guides claim were placed in mayonnaise jars, in a crypt not far from the castle. According to his instructions, the spot was covered in poison ivy. However, despite the fortification, someone broke in to the burial chamber, smashed one of the mayo jars with a cat mummy, and stole Hammond's head. A ransom was paid and the skull was eventually returned.

The castle, complete with pipe organ, drawbridge, and a dungeon, is open to the public at 80 Hesperus Avenue in Gloucester. Directions and hours of operation are available at www.hammondcastle.org or by calling (978) 283-7673.

DANCES WITH WOLVES. NOT.
Ipswich

If Little Red Riding Hood had traveled to Wolf Hollow, she would have learned a lot more than Grandma without having to take a single step into the forest. Wolf Hollow was founded in Ipswich in 1988 to allow people to experience wolves in the animals' natural habitat and to dispel the many myths surrounding the much-maligned creatures.

Wild wolves once populated all forty-eight continental U.S. states. Today they're endangered in forty-seven of those states. Humans are the wolves' only predators. The North American Wolf Foundation, which runs Wolf Hollow, contends that the wolf can harmoniously co-exist with humans and other mammals; it is a matter of understanding wolf behavior and the pack's social order. According to the Foundation, there is not a single documented case of a healthy wild wolf attacking a human. But just in case, the pack at Wolf Hollow is enclosed in a large meadow protected by a 12-foot-high chain fence. Visitors are cautioned not to stare a wolf in the eye or to show their teeth. The founders of Wolf Hollow, the late Paul Soffron and his wife, Joni, learned firsthand the laws of the pack. They even slept with young pups to create a lifetime bond.

Wolf Hollow is open year-round and there are one-hour structured presentations, weather permitting. Check ahead. There are also special seminars and events such as one observance that poet Allen Ginsberg might have enjoyed, "Howl Night." Grandma never had it so good.

Wolf Hollow is about 3 miles east of Ipswich on Route 133. For more information call (978) 356–0216 or visit www.wolf hollowipswich.com.

HEY, IF THE SHOE FITS. . .
Lowell

Lowell is perhaps best known as the home of beat-generation author Jack Kerouac. But if you are on the road looking for something lowbrow but upbeat and find yourself in the historic mill town, drop by the Lowell Historical Society. There you will find two curious items that have almost nothing to do with Lowell history.

The first is a helmet made out of a coconut and a sea urchin. It was worn by a Lowell soldier who served in the Philippine Insurrection of 1899–1901. The second item is a mummified ankle and foot. No one seems to know how the preserved appendage got to the museum, where it came from, or what it really is. Until a few years ago, it was thought to be a mummified child's foot from ancient Egypt, but recently an expert identified it as being from South America and perhaps belonging to a woman.

Both items are in storage but are taken out on special occasions. The Historical Society is located at the Boote Cotton Mills Museum, 400 Foot of John Street in Lowell. (No, we're not kidding, and no, it's not John's foot. That's just the address.)

D U N G E O N   R O C K
L y n n

L egend has it that in 1658 pirate Thomas Veal sailed up the Saugus River and anchored at Pirate's Glen. Although three of his buccaneers were captured and hung by British soldiers, Veal escaped into the woods and hid in a cave all alone with a stash of ill-gotten gains. Suddenly a violent earthquake shook Lynn, entombing Veal and sealing his treasure trove in what has come to be called Dungeon Rock.

Over the centuries there have been numerous attempts by psychics and the certifiably insane to recover the loot. The most famous attempt began in 1852, when Hiram Marble, a spiritualist from Charlton, Massachusetts, his wife, and his son Edwin, purchased five acres of land in the area and, "guided by the spirit of revelation," started digging for the hidden treasure.

Dungeon Rock is the site of two graves and pirate's treasure.
Photo courtesy of Dan Small

To help raise money for their project, the Marbles gave tours of the site and sold bonds for a dollar each, promising investors a share of the loot. The Marbles also sought guidance from the spirit of Pirate Veal, who perhaps advised the abrupt changes in direction apparent in the tunnel today. It is more likely that the spirits assured the Marbles that, like Moses wandering the desert for forty years, it was necessary for them to toil before reaching their reward.

Hiram Marble died in 1868. His son continued digging until his own death, in 1880. By that time the duo had dug 145 feet through solid rock, a rate of about a foot a month. Edwin's last wish, to be buried at Dungeon Rock, was granted. You will find a large pink rock at the top of a set of stairs next to an old cellar hole marking his grave.

While the gravel debris from the Marbles' blasting and remnants from many structures they built in the area can still be seen, the pirate treasure, if there ever was any, remains to be found.

Curiously, the Marbles were not seeking the treasure for themselves. Their first goal was to prove that the dead could communicate from the afterlife. They didn't have much luck there. Hiram Marble also hoped to use the pirate's treasure to purchase land in the area for the people of Lynn to enjoy forever. He largely succeeded. Soon after Edwin's death the city of Lynn purchased the family's land for their new park, the Lynn Woods.

The entrance to Dungeon Tunnel is sealed with an iron gate but open to the public from May through October and by request. Bring a flashlight; it's really dark and scary.

In late October the Friends of Lynn Woods hold a Dungeon Rock Day celebration, where people dress as pirates and tell stories.

The shortest walk to Dungeon Rock is from the Rose Garden entrance to Lynn Woods. Maps are available at the entrance. For more information, check out the Lynn Woods Reservation Guide at www.flw.org or call the rangers at (781) 477–7123.

THE GOD MACHINE
Lynn

T he era of the 1850s was a high-water mark for spiritualists in the United States, and High Rock, with its commanding view of Boston to the south, was something of a magnet for séances and spiritualists. Molly Pitcher, said to be clairvoyant, lived at the base of High Rock until her death in 1813. She was legendary among sailors whose fortunes she foretold before they set sail. In 1846 a man named Jesse Hutchinson bought High Rock and erected Stone Cottage on the side of the hill. It became home to Hutchinson and his eleven brothers and sisters, who formed the world-famous group the Hutchinson Family Singers. Jesse Hutchinson was a social activist and spiritualist who organized a meeting of spirit-minded people on High Rock. Reportedly, in 1852 spirits from twenty-four countries gathered on the mound. A year later nineteenth-century spiritualist John Murray Spear made the High Rock scene.

Although many say High Rock is as close to heaven as a Lynn poet can get, it obviously wasn't close enough for Spear.

In 1853 Spear and a group of philanthropic spirits he called the "Band of Electricizers" gathered atop the 170-foot-tall granite hill to build "Heaven's last, best gift to man." They set about constructing the New Messiah.

The Electricizers, led by the spirit of Benjamin Franklin, provided Spear and his followers with step-by-step instructions to build the New Messiah. It was later dubbed the God Machine.

Slowly the God Machine took shape on a dining room table. It was a mass of metal spheres, magnets, and coils of zinc and copper. There was a flywheel in the center of the contraption, with wire connections. When it was complete Spear encased himself in a shroud of metal plates and gemstones and for about an hour came in contact with the machine. Not much happened, although later a follower of Spear's went into labor while touching the God Machine, even though she claimed she wasn't pregnant. Spear insisted that at the moment of the baby's birth the machine became animate for an instant.

The contraption was later dismantled and moved to upstate New York, where an angry mob of nonbelievers reportedly mauled and mangled the God Machine. No trace of it has ever been found.

Today High Rock is still a place for those looking toward the heavens. Atop the tower built on the summit in 1906 are an observatory and a new computerized telescope. The observatory is open to the public on Tuesday nights or by appointment for large groups. For more information visit www.ci.lynn.ma.us/public_documents/lynnma_resources/highrock27.

To get to High Rock, take Essex Street and make a left on Rockaway Street. Turn up High Rock Street to Circuit Avenue and park at the end of Circuit.

CARRYING A TUNE IN A BUCKET
Manchester-By-the-Sea

D inah Shore it's not, but Singing Beach really does sing . . . sort of. Shuffle your feet over the sand or pull your hands through it quickly and you'll hear a squeaking sound, not unlike a high-pitched violin (or Dinah on a bad day.) To get the full experience, try the sand closest to the bathhouse. It seems to be the most mellifluous.

Naturalist and writer Henry David Thoreau wrote about the sonorous sands of Manchester-By-the-Sea in the mid-nineteenth century, but scientists are still not sure of the exact mechanism of its tonal quality. It's thought that the uniform size and round shape of the grains is responsible for the phenomenon. Whatever the cause, even if you could never carry a tune in a bucket, now you can.

Singing Beach is at the end of Masconomo Street off Route 127 in Manchester-By-the-Sea. Parking is limited to town residents with special stickers, so you will have to park your car in town about a half-mile away and walk to the concert that awaits you.

BILLIONS OF SWEET NOTHINGS
Revere

Back in the 1920s there were at least thirty-two candy manufacturers in the Boston area churning out sweet stuff by the megaton. One is still going strong. The New England Confectionery Company, or NECCO, recently celebrated its 150th anniversary, making it the oldest continuously operating candy company in the United States.

Until 2003 NECCO was located in a huge building next to the MIT campus in Cambridge. It was the largest factory in the world whose entire space was devoted to candy production. The company has since moved to Revere, north of Boston.

NECCO is literally a sweetheart of a company. Besides its signature Necco Wafers, it produces eight billion Sweethearts Conversation Hearts a year. They're the chalky-tasting, heart-shaped candies bearing saccharine sayings such as "Kiss Me," "Be True," and "Be Mine."

The Valentine's Day amore mottos have been updated in recent years to include "Girl Power," "Swing Time," and "Got Love." For a minimum order of $7,600, you can even have a custom-made cupid-saying printed on the hearts. You will have a whole lot of loving to go around. That's about 1.6 million candy hearts.

EXTRA! EXTRA! READ ALL ABOUT IT!
Rockport

At 52 Pigeon Hill Street in Rockport is an unusual home you not only can read about; you can actually read the home itself.

The house and most of the furnishings are built out of old newspapers. Elis F. Stenman constructed the house as a hobby. Perhaps his talent for paper construction had something to do with being a mechanical engineer who built machines to make paper clips. Certainly he had a passion for newspapers. He read three a day.

In 1922 Stenman started experimenting with newspapers as insulation for the cottage he was constructing. The material proved so strong that he decided to varnish it. The outer walls are 215 pages thick, and the roof is lined with newspapers but has a wood outer shell. It took Stenman two years to build the house and eighteen years to construct the clock, chairs, tables, and piano that furnish it. Although the fireplace is made of bricks, the mantelpiece is built from the magazine sections of Sunday newspapers.

The Paper House is located at 52 Pigeon Hill Street in Pigeon Cove in Rockport. Take Route 127 to Pigeon Cove; after the Yankee Clipper Inn, take the second left onto Curtis Street and then turn left onto Pigeon Hill Street. On Curtis Street you will see handwritten signs on telephone poles directing you to the house. Of course, they're written on paper.

Visitors are on the honor system to make a contribution. To read an interview with Elis Stenman, go to www.rockportusa .com/paperhouse/.

The Paper House is black and white and read all over.

Photo by Bruce Gellerman

ROUTE 1:
THE (R)ODE TO INDIVIDUALITY
Saugus

Ten miles north of Boston you will find a major dose of road-side America circa 1960. The strip of Route 1 stretching from Saugus to Peabody is a six-lane tabernacle to garish taste and unbridled individuality. It is a road that tells it like it was; a time when your mother wore a bouffant, your dad motored happily with a tiger in his gas tank, and the family saw the U.S.A. in a Chevrolet. You'll want to yell, "Hi dad, hi mom, hi Beaver" as you pass the Bel-Aire diner and the Fern Motel, a place Norman Bates would feel right at home. And if you want to whack a few balls, stop at Route 1 Miniature Golf, where an orange Tyrannosaurus Rex, a national landmark, guards the links.

In its heyday, Route 1 had more restaurants per mile, serving more people, than anywhere else in the nation. The eateries were an exuberant celebration of tacky taste and entrepreneurial chutzpah, and the road was a mecca for marketing meals run amok. Different was better. Biggest was best.

Atop a hill overlooking Route 1 in Saugus, you can still see the huge pagoda-shaped Weylus, once said to be the largest Chinese restaurant on the planet. It featured cuisine from every Chinese canton in a style you might call "Saugus Early-Elvis Dynasty." They could serve up egg foo yung for 1,400 with no sweat. Alas, the last egg roll left the Weylus kitchen in the late 1990s. But fear not; you won't go hungry along the Route 1 kitschway today. If you have a hankering for a slab of beef the size of Plymouth Rock, you can still head to the Hilltop Steakhouse, the place with the 68-foot neon cactus right next to the giant plastic grazing cows. Feel like Italian? A bit

The 30-foot-tall Hilltop Steak House cactus.
Photo by Bruce Gellerman

The two-masted Weathervane restaurant.
Photo by Bruce Gellerman

farther north is Prince Restaurant. It's the one with the three-story LEANING TOWER OF PIZZA sign, just across the road from Kowloon, a humongous grass-hut Polynesian restaurant with giant Tiki statues out front and a bubbling volcano inside. Diners looking for a nautical motif can chart a course a bit farther north to the life-sized, two-masted Weathervane restaurant. The "ship" is anchored between a Yankee Candle Shop and a Christmas Tree Shop. Guiding the way is a faux lighthouse in the parking lot. You can't miss it.

Yet despite the best efforts of kitsch preservationists, this roadway—architecturally littered with a kind of joyful abandon you just don't find much anymore—is slowly but surely giving way to staid chain stores and look-alike fast-food franchises. Nonetheless, there is enough of the old Route 1 still standing to make a trip down memory lane at forty miles an hour worth it. Just hop in your Chevy, put the top down, turn up Dean Martin on the AM radio, and cruise the road. It's *amore*.

HEY, BARTENDER, I'LL HAVE ANOTHER ONE OF THOSE MEDICINES
Tewksbury

In the old administration building of what is now known as Tewksbury Hospital is the only public health museum in the United States.

The hospital was established in 1852 as an almshouse for the poor. Its most famous patient during the nineteenth century was Anne Sullivan, later the tutor and companion of Helen Keller. In 1994 the bottom floor was converted into the unique public health museum by Chet Kennedy, former art director for the Massachusetts Department of Public Health, "to show to the world what a great heritage we have in this part of

*The Public Health Museum's collection of patent
medicines might not be good for what ails you.*
Photo by Bruce Gellerman

the country" and to sing the praises of public health pioneers.
Colonial Massachusetts passed the first laws to register births
and deaths; it was the first state to require lead testing in children; and it was the first with a tuberculosis hospital. It's hard
to remember now that in 1900 TB was a major cause of death
in the United States.

The Queen-Anne-style museum building itself is an exhibit, listed on the National Register of Historic Places. The eight rooms in the museum include a nurses' classroom and a hospital room from the 1920s. The Mural Room features a four-wall mural from the Works Progress Administration in the 1930s. The steep staircase up one wall leads to a little room used to store records of venereal disease.

Massachusetts was also the epicenter for the patent medicine industry, as evidenced by the museum's extensive collection of bottles and advertisements. Included are bottles of Turtle's Elixir, Atwood's Jaundice Bitters, and Bee's Laxative Cough Syrup. Prominently displayed are patent medicines produced by Lydia Pinkham. In 1876 Pinkham began manufacturing her nostrum, Lydia E. Pinkham's Vegetable Compound, in nearby Lynn promising to cure "the worst form of 'Female Complaints'—everything from 'General Debility' to cancer." The elixir was based on a formula Pinkham's husband won in a card game. Lydia Pinkham became known as "a lady's best friend" during Prohibition, and no wonder: The elixir was 90 percent alcohol.

Pinkham's cure-all was a phenomenon and her salesmanship made her one of the most successful women in U.S. history. Indeed, although she died in 1883, customers were still encouraged to write to Mrs. Pinkham for medical advice. In 1905, twenty-two years after her death and countless letters later, the *Ladies' Home Journal* exposed the scam in an article that included a photograph of Mrs. P's tombstone, located at the Pine Grove Cemetery in Lynn within sight of the maintenance garage, 145 Boston Street.

The Public Health Museum in Massachusetts is located off Interstate 93 at exit 42 West. More information is available at the museum Web site, www.publichealthmuseum.org.

What's a Knight Like You Doing in a Place Like This?
Westford

Historian Frederick J. Pohls says "fuggetabout" Columbus sailing the ocean blue in 1492. In his book, *Atlantic Crossings Before Columbus,* Pohls makes the case that it was a seafaring Scot in 1398 who first "discovered" America. According to Pohls' research, Henry Sinclair (Earl of Rosslyn, Prince of Orkney and Lord of Shetland, Duke of Oldenburg and Premier Earl of Norway) set out to explore newly discovered Newfoundland but wound up getting chased away by natives. It seems he then got caught in a New England Nor'easter, sending Sinclair's armada to the coast just north of Boston, where he had better luck with the local inhabitants. Maybe it was all his titles, or maybe it was his kilt. In any case, Sinclair and his crew of one hundred were allowed to spend the winter on shore. In the spring they trooped inland and climbed what is now called Prospect Hill in Westford, perhaps seeking a place to hide the Holy Grail some say they carried with them. Historian Pohls writes that one of Prince Henry's men died there and the Scots memorialized him by carving a marker into a flat, 8-foot-square hunk of granite. Although the weatherworn carving is faint, you might be able to make out a roughly life-sized portrayal of a fourteenth-century knight with a sword, shield, and crest, wearing a helmet.

"Holy Grail, shmoly grail," say nonbelievers who contend that the Westford Knight is nothing but a weather-beaten rock. Decide for yourself. From the Westford Common, make a right on Lincoln Street onto Main Street and a left onto Depot Street. Park near the Abbot School and walk 50 yards up Depot. A commemorative marble marker marks the spot where Prince Henry may have left evidence of his discovery of the New World, or maybe not.

THE SCOOP ON THE BATTLESHIP MAINE
Woburn

Do you remember the *Maine*? The USS *Maine* was the battleship that mysteriously blew up in Havana Harbor in 1898, setting off the Spanish–American War. To remember more, go to Main Street in Woburn, where you'll find remains of the *Maine*, specifically one of the ship's ventilator cowls (an air scoop that looks like a crushed tuba and is enshrined in a glass case).

When residents of Woburn had requested a piece of the *Maine* in 1911, Congress rejected them, stating that only non-profit, patriotic organizations could apply. The citizens got Local Post 161 of the Grand Army of the Republic to submit an application, and it was approved by Congress. The 315-pound, barnacle-encrusted cowl was put on display in the front window of Whitcher's Drug Store (now a sushi restaurant) on Main Street. A year later it was encased on the Common and dedicated on July 4, 1913.

As they say, "from sea to shining sea."

Visitors can remember the Maine *on Main Street in Woburn.*

Photo by Bruce Gellerman

SOUTHEAST MASSACHUSETTS
AND THE CAPE AND ISLANDS

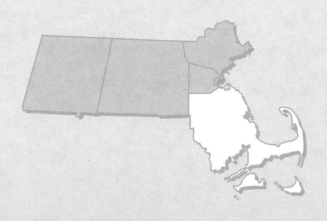

SOUTHEAST MASSACHUSETTS AND THE CAPE AND ISLANDS

I'M DREAMING OF A LIGHT CHRISTMAS
Attleboro

If you are of a certain age and cultural background, you spent many youthful hours among cloaked figures—silent, swift, certain. We're talking nuns here, those powerful and virtually omniscient harbingers of order, guilt, and swift retribution. Also of humor, teaching, an understanding ear, and a mean swing on the softball field. It all depends—hardly surprising—on the individual. But uniforms can be deceiving and even leveling. Part of the raiment, at least in the Northeast in the 1960s, was strands of rosary beads, which are a physical system for tracking a series of prayers, like a spiritual abacus. In those days, when you were six, those beads seemed large, far bigger than marbles. In Attleboro at the La Salette Shrine, however, you will find a rosary that dwarfs those once sported by the nuns, with beads as big as bowling balls. The site, originally intended to be a sanatorium, was purchased in 1919 by the Methodist Church. It was called Attleboro Springs, named for the springs on the property. The Methodists used it as a

At Christmas, visitors enjoy the lighter part of the shrine.
Photo by Erik Sherman

retreat for a time, finally closing the facility in 1938. In 1942
representatives from a French Catholic order called the Mis-
sionaries of Our Lady of La Salette bought the property and,
ten years later, began building a shrine commemorating a supposed appearance of Mary to two children in France. The Giant
Rosary, which stretches over a walkway arch, is part of the
scene, as are other religious statues and peaceful gardens.

A particularly bright and uplifting time to visit is during
the annual Christmas Festival of Lights. Tens of thousands of
miniature lights illuminate the trees and grounds and draw
hundreds of thousands of visitors. The lights go on at 5:00 P.M.
from Thanksgiving through the first few days of January. To
see the beads and lights, follow the blue-and-white signs on
Route 152 in Attleboro or from Exit 5 on Route 95. For more
information, visit http://lasalette.shrine.tripod.com.

AMERICAN GRAFFITI
Berkley

K ids who "tag"—draw large and elaborate versions of graffiti on anything that doesn't move (and on some things that do, if you look at subways in New York)—might think they are on the cutting edge of generational revolt. Oh, if only they realized that the graffiti in this land even makes their parents look young. Dighton Rock is a noted bit of sediment: an 11-foot boulder covered in petroglyphs (fancy talk for lines carved into a rock) that was originally on the Taunton River at Berkley. Think that urban tagging can be hard to read? These ancient inscriptions were left by unknown people with a meaning that is more obscure than a political party's press release. Back in 1712, when Cotton Mather wasn't looking for witches, he was trying to figure out what the markings meant. He even made a copy of the figures and sent them to the Royal Society in London for a translation, but the experts there were undecided.

Was this the literary equivalent of crop circles and mysterious Mayan hieroglyphs? It could be that what you can see is actually the musings of an international group of ancient punks. Over the years many have argued that the petroglyphs aren't a single language, but several. Some scholars think that they have deciphered bits and pieces. One of those pieces is the name *Thorfinn Karlsefni* and the phrase, "Miguel Cortereal by will of God, here Chief of the Indians," along with the date 1511 and a Portuguese coat-of-arms. (Not all students of language and history agree with even these fragmentary—or is it figmentary?—translations.) What is clear, however, is that Dighton Rock became a veritable billboard for graffiti enthusiasts over many years. To avoid having the rock face damaged by tides and weather and the modern tagging practitioner, it now sits in a museum in Dighton Rock State Park.

We have our own theories on what was meant by the writing. Either this is an old variation of *Kilroy was here,* or an early comic dramatic masterpiece, *Dighton Beach Memoirs.* If you visit, be sure to bring a picnic lunch for the eighty-five acres of grassy areas and shade trees. There is also boating, fishing, and hiking. Dighton Rock State Park is on Bay View Avenue; for more information, call (508) 822–7537 or visit www.state.ma.us/dem/parks/digr.htm.

A LASTING IMPRESSION
Brockton

I melda Marcos has nothing on the city of Brockton when it comes to shoes. She only had hundreds of pairs at hand (or would that be "at foot?") But the Brockton Shoe Museum lifts shoe obsession to an art. Those who are interested in fashion—whether leather or lace—can see how boots and sneakers can be a veritable foundation for a look. Not only does this shoe showplace examine the footwear-making craft from the sixteenth century on, but it also has entire theme collections, like military shoes from the Civil War to Desert Storm. If your mother wore combat boots, they may be here.

Then there are the celebrity shoes, including those worn by Ted Williams, Arthur Fiedler, and Rocky Marciano. (Marciano was a Brockton native.) There is even a pair, size twenty-four, used by an Italian boxer of the 1930s. And don't forget those of the political persuasion: Mamie Eisenhower, President Gerald Ford, and President Bill Clinton, whose sneakers are fast enough to get out of almost any scrape. If you get tired of Shoes, the Exhibit, then you can move on to Shoes, the Movie—actually, a video of shoes. We won't be heels and give the end-

The Brockton Shoe Museum features the size 24 shoes worn by
1930s world champion Italian boxer Primo Carnera.
Photo by Erik Sherman

ing away. But we do have a bone to pick with the people who
have designed the attraction's marketing message. The Shoe
Museum bills itself as "the only authentic shoe museum in
America." We beg to differ and offer as evidence the closets of
virtually all the women we have ever known. You can judge for
yourself at the Brockton Heritage Center, 216 North Pearl
Street. For more information, or to find out if they have your
size, visit www.brocktonma.com/bhs/shoe.html or call (508)
583–1039.

HEAVY LIGHTHOUSE
Cohasset

W hoever said that watching over a lighthouse was easy work, let alone even safe? Sure, turn the switch on and turn it off—and make out your last will and testament. Just off the coast of Cohasset is Minot's Ledge Light. Erected in the mid-nineteenth century, it is the most wave-swept lighthouse of the United States Lighthouse System (USLHS). This is the Hawaii of the lighthouse set, where the biggest and baddest waves break—and, sometimes, so do the light keepers. After the lighthouse's initial construction, the first keeper complained about how dangerous the waves were and immediately quit. The next keeper also complained. The year after the lighthouse went up, it came down in an April storm, killing the two assistants who were on duty. The USLHS wanted a light there, since this was a dangerous stretch of water, so it rebuilt on the site. Some people can't take no for an answer. Replacing the building was quite the trick, using 1,079 blocks of granite from Quincy—more than 3,500 tons in all—cut to fit together like a well-made joint on a dresser drawer. It took the USLHS five years to put all the blocks in place. Impressive, but the engineering wonder still left keepers wondering why, in the name of all that was holy, they should sit out there. People quit, right and left—that is, when they didn't become violent or literally lose their minds. Reports of hauntings include the mysterious polishing of lenses, odd noises, and a figure screaming in Portuguese for help while hanging off a ladder. Talk about your hostile working environments.

Amusingly, the Minot's Ledge Light is also known as the "I love you" light, because it flashes in a 1–4–3 pattern, mirroring the number of letters in each word. (Imagine what conditions would have been like if it hated you.)

The memorial of the Minot's Ledge Light honors the
two men who died when the lighthouse collapsed.
Photo by Erik Sherman

These days the lighthouse itself is automated, working off solar power, and is closed to the public. The lighthouse keeper's abode has become a private club and a pleasant venue for functions. But you can read about the storm and the men who died (although not the ones who went off the deep end, so to speak) by going to the memorial at Cohasset Harbor. The memorial includes a replica of the top portion of the lighthouse on granite blocks from the original structure. The light keepers' residence also makes an interesting place for a social gathering. Set sail for a driveway that runs off Border Street, next to the small bridge.

LADY OF THE LIGHTHOUSE

Working in a lighthouse was always a lonely job, perhaps making the appearance of ghosts not all that unwelcome. Maybe previous occupants didn't want the new ones to feel isolated. One such place is Plymouth Light, formerly known as Gurnet Light, established in 1768 on the property of John and Hannah Thomas at the tip of Duxbury Beach. It was one of a dozen colonial stations and John was the lighthouse keeper until he was killed during the Revolutionary War. That left Hannah as the first official female lighthouse keeper on the continent. According to accounts at the time, Hannah was good at what she did. She was also very loyal, refusing to leave the lighthouse during her life. She worked until her death, at which point her son took over. The original lighthouse is long gone, having been replaced in 1803, rebuilt in 1843, and then rebuilt again in 1924.

In 1994 Bob and Sandra Shanklin, world-famous lighthouse photographers, enthusiasts, and authors, came to photograph the building and stayed at the keeper's house. In the middle of the night, Bob woke and saw the apparition of a woman's face, dark clothing, and shoulder-length hair. Could Hannah be the lighthouse keeper emeritus?

Although Plymouth is technically the closest city to the lighthouse, the only way to approach is by four-wheel-drive or by foot from Duxbury Beach. The lighthouse is generally closed to the public, though it is open on such special occasions as the annual Opening of the Bay each May in Duxbury.

GOOD WORKS AND GOOD EATS
Eastham

*S*aving souls is serious work, but that doesn't mean that you can't have some fun while you do it. The Methodists have long understood that part of spiritual development was being in the proper atmosphere, and they have been drawn to beautiful seaside areas in the hot days of summer. In Eastham is Millennium Grove, an oak grove in which as many as 5,000 of the faithful would camp and pray with some 150 ministers. Henry David Thoreau witnessed this on one of his walking trips of the Cape and later wrote about it. While it's easy to build an image of what this must have been like, it's easy for that image to be wrong. Life at the camp was not one of deprivation; the worshipers were apparently open to sustaining the flesh as well as the spirit. Thoreau wrote of his visit: "I saw the heaps of clamshells left under the tables, where they had feasted in previous summers, and supposed, of course, that that was the work of the unconverted, or the backsliders and scoffers. It looked as if a camp-meeting must be a singular combination of a prayer-meeting and a picnic." We can only imagine the difficulties the faithful must have faced: mounds of shellfish and not a drop of melted butter in sight. To get a feel for the old surroundings, let the spirit move you to Campground Road and look for the old lobster bibs.

DIGGING CULTURE
Easton

If you liked watching *Home Improvement,* or if going to
Home Depot is your idea of a night out on the town, then
the Arnold B. Tofias Industrial Archives at Stonehill College
will give you fun by the spadeful. This special collection of
the school's Stonehill Industrial History Center, located in the
Cushing-Martin Building on the campus, is nicknamed the
Shovel Museum. There's a good reason for the moniker, as this
could well be the largest historic retrospective of that most
essential icon of earth movement. It's not to everyone's taste;
according to a researcher, in 1995 only 200 people visited the
collection. What do most people think it must be, a hole in the
ground? Absolutely not: There are papers—diaries, sales
ledgers, and catalogs—of the O. Ames Company, which happened to make shovels. And you will also find more than 800
shovels and shovel components, as well as trowels, trenchers,
and other related tools.

The business had its start in the Revolutionary War, when
Capt. John Ames, a blacksmith by trade, made shovels and
muskets in West Bridgewater. His son moved the business to
an abandoned nail factory in Easton in 1803. Because merchan-
dise from England was relatively cheap, Ames concentrated on
making expensive, high-quality shovels. The company thrived
in Easton until it merged with another in the 1950s and moved
out of town. In the process of the move, the new owners managed to leave an attic full of shovels in the old building. Thus
was born the collection. Family members are still in the area,
and one donated the paperwork a few years ago. A gallery is
open where you can view the shovels through glass, but if you

More than 800 shovels and shovel components are
displayed at Stonehill College.
Photo by Erik Sherman

want to dig into the subject more, call the curator at (508) 565–1403 to arrange for a walk through the *objets d'dirt,* or visit www.stonehill.edu/archives/sihc. The historical big dig is at the Cushing-Martin Building, Stonehill College, 320 Washington Street.

Pop-Top Art
East Taunton

College students who spend their hours hardly studying and partying heartily might seem to be wasting important intellectually formative years. Yet we'd like to think that an entire genre of beer art has been the result. Unlike much cultural philanthropy, this is not a category that owes much to wealthy patrons or even government underwriting. Beer art is something that the average person on the street supports, sip by sip. There are the nameless people who have done their small share, and then there are the heroic figures who, each like a modern Hercules, move and direct the rivers of frothy liquid. It is the latter category that features the East Taunton Beer Can and Breweriana Museum. Kevin "Kevbo" Logan, the owner and curator, was introduced to this collection pastime by his cousin in Galveston, Texas. Since then Kevin has collected more than 1,000 cans, along with roughly the same number of coasters, half a dozen beer trays, and assorted glasses and bottles from around the world. His best find was in 1980, cleaning out a woman's basement; she told him to keep anything he found. In an old running refrigerator were two rare Schaeffer 1964 World's Fair Special Steel Flattops, one of which now sits in the museum. (The other went to cousin Patrick, a belated but much welcomed, we assume, thank-you.) On his Web site, Kevin answers what might seem obvious: Why would someone collect beer cans? "Beer cans are pretty fascinating, really." We are sure that the display-preparation phase, which includes draining the contents (from the bottom) doesn't hurt. In fact, it's probably good for what ales you. The collection is large, but the number of visitors is only about forty a year. To arrange a visit or just to take a virtual tour, go to http://kevslog.tripod.com/beercanmuseum—it's the yeast you could do.

SHELL GAME
Fall River

The USS *Massachusetts* never lost a sailor in combat but the government nearly lost the *Massachusetts*. In the early 1960s the Navy was going to sell the battleship—home to 2,300 sailors during World War II—for scrap. The ship, built in 1941 in the city of Quincy, Massachusetts, had joined the War in November 1942. In a battle with the ship *Jean Bart* during the

Battleship Cove is home to the world's largest collection of historic naval ships, including the USS Massachusetts.
Photo by Erik Sherman

drive into North Africa, the *Massachusetts* let loose the war's first American 16-inch shell. (This piece of artillery was nothing to trifle with—it was nearly a foot and a half in diameter.) On August 9, 1945, less than a month before the end of the war in Asia, the *Massachusetts* shelled the Kamaishi, Honshu, ironworks with, as it turns out, what were probably the War's last American 16-inch shells.

Luckily, before the Navy could sell the *Massachusetts*, a group of citizens organized a battle plan and turned the valiant ship into a museum worthy of the name. They rescued not only the *Massachusetts*, but an entire fleet, adding a destroyer, a submarine, two PT boats, a mechanized landing craft, and even some foreign craft, such as a Russian warship and a Japanese suicide-attack boat. Now the *Massachusetts* hosts camping adventures where youth groups can see what a sailor's life was like. That includes meals served on board, berthing in crew's quarters, movies about Navy ships and Navy life, and Morse code classes for those who want to join the signal corps and pursue radio licenses. There are even facilities for functions and meetings for those above the recruitment age. Stop by headquarters at Battleship Cove; the Web site www.battleshipcove .com gives directions, hours of operation, and other details.

A H ATCHET J OB
Fall River

F orget television movie re-creations of sensational crimes or even reality shows. If you have an ax to grind with secondhand titillation, you might find a trip to the Lizzie Borden Bed and Breakfast Museum intriguing. This was the site of the double-hatchet murder of Andrew J. and Abby Borden and the trial of their spinster daughter, Lizzie. Legal authorities not

The old Borden house is now a bed-and-breakfast.
Photo by Erik Sherman

only charged Lizzie with the murder of each parent, but they also accused her of an additional charge of killing both of them—sort of a double double-homicide.

Lizzie was tried and eventually acquitted—whether fair or not we couldn't say, as that would be splitting hairs. But much of the defense's success seemed to lie in excluding testimony Borden gave during the inquest that contradicted what she said at the trial, as well as having certain other testimony labeled inadmissible. Oh, and there was that mysterious man who had been hanging around the Borden home. No matter about the verdict, though, as the town didn't forgive her. That rhyme about "giving her mother forty whacks and when she was done giving her father forty-one" had to hurt, and it was untrue—mom got nineteen and dad, only eleven.

Now, thanks to the time-honored commercial tool of exploiting the macabre, you can experience the Borden house up close and personal by spending the night in the very dwelling that was the site of the deeds. You can even have a suite that includes Lizzie's room. The meal portion is actually similar, so we read, to the ones the Borden parents had the morning of that . . . uh . . . unfortunate incident: bananas and jonny-cakes, washed down with coffee and sugar cookies.

There are tours of the house on weekends in May and June, and daily in July and August, but the hours vary. For more information, go to www.lizzie-borden.com or call (508) 675-7333. To reach that (hopefully not) final resting place, go to 92 Second Street.

OLD TECH

*I*s he a curator, or simply a pack rat? We're not sure, but Mark Vess of Hanson certainly has come up with the best excuse for keeping an overwhelmingly large collection of old stuff. Calling his obsession with antiquated technology a "museum" seems unfair. After all, it's not a public institution and you can't drop by to see it. But the founder and curator does give a few tours each year to school groups and collectors.

Vess started saving old radios and phones when he was a child, and if his own mother couldn't stop him, who can? Now, decades later, he keeps the bulk of the collection in the hayloft of his barn, though it does spill out into other parts of the house, and some things—a tractor, a number of antique autos, and a player one-man band (piano with other instruments)—require a bit more space planning.

A number of the items, such as the Edison wind-up phonograph and the manual typewriters, are obvious in their function . . . or they would be, for those old enough to remember records and carbon paper. Then there are things that could use descriptive panels, like the electrical coils that doctors of the late-nineteenth century used to (unsuccessfully) treat stomach aches and bad pregnancies. But not everything is hand-powered: Vess also has a selection of handheld transistor radios. Those lucky enough to tour past the wooden display tables will also see cameras, flashlights, telegraph keys, light bulbs, sewing machines, and even antique shaving blades. The world may be waiting for a better mouse trap, but when society moves on, you can bet that Mark Vess will have the old model.

R EADY O AR N OT
Hull

M ost museums are happy with just telling about the past. The Hull Lifesaving Museum does that and goes a bit further, though with a twist. The U.S. Life Saving Service, established in the 1870s to assist mariners in distress, had stations up and down the East Coast, and the branch in Hull was certainly busy. But the present-day museum actually has a program for putting people into the water, not taking them out. It sponsors various open-water rowing races, and you have to wonder about the conditions when you hear some of the names: the Snow Row and the Icebreaker. (Undoubtedly the museum staff doesn't have to worry about people falling out of the pilot boats, dories, wherries, and whale boats, as they would probably just bounce off the frozen surface.)

If you don't catch one of the races, there is still a lot to see—and to think about. This part of the state has had a long relationship with the sea, and the loss of life in its waters has been real and historic. Sometimes the rescuers from the local station would take boats out to pull mariners from the rough waters off the shore. When the weather was too rough, a canon would shoot a ball and line out to sea so those in trouble could pull themselves back to land (if they were lucky).

The Hull Lifesaving Museum is open year-round and has both artifacts and hands-on exhibits. Be sure to go up into the children's space and climb into the cupola, which, on a clear day, offers a view of the harbor and the neighboring lighthouse that can't be beat. Row, row, row your way to 1117 Nantasket Avenue. Just don't forget your life preserver. For information, call (781) 925–5433, or go to www.bostonharborheritage.org/main.htm.

DIZZY DISPLAYS
Hull

Ever feel like you're going around in circles? It's an unpleasant hazard of modern life. Instead of giving up, try a little sublimation: Head to the end of the small boardwalk-like strip in Hull, and check out of the rat race and into childhood at the Paragon Carousel. Before the turn of the twentieth century, this area was a major New England resort, complete with an amusement park. In 1928 its owners installed this carousel, number eighty-five of the eighty-nine built by the Philadelphia Toboggan Company, known for its realistic hand-carved figures. Back in those days Hull was a resort town, and people would flock to the shore to enjoy a vacation in the cool breezes. Times changed, and the seaside community became a bit run-down. It transformed into a blue-collar residential area as plane travel became more prevalent and could take the wealthy to real tropical destinations. The Paragon Amusement Park, long a fixture, finally came down in the mid-1980s, the victim of a condominium development. Most of the history is just a paper memory, but thanks to the efforts of community activists and sentimental supporters, three investors purchased the carousel and set it up on land provided by the state. Fate does have a way of going in circles, and the owners decided that they wanted "off" the merry-go-round when their interests changed. They put the carousel on the market again, and it appeared that it was going to be dismantled and sold piecemeal to antiques buyers. Rather than let the beloved amusement be taken for a ride, its fans from neighboring towns raised more than a million dollars to purchase the carousel and save it for posterity. Today the carousel's mighty Wurlitzer band organ plays on. The sixty-six wooden horses and two Roman chariots

The carousel in Hull is a mechanized taste of
summer, whether you ride or watch.
Photo by Erik Sherman

have been taking turns undergoing restoration, and today they await to take you away from care. Just hop on and enjoy the satisfyingly long ride. Next to the carousel is a great local ice cream store, and the beach across the street has its own appeal, as long as you aren't horsing around. The carousel is at 205 Nantasket Avenue; call (781) 925–0472 or visit www.enjoy-hull.com for information.

GRAVE ENTERTAINMENT
Hyannis

Most people think you need a campfire, dirt, and mosquitoes for a good ghost story. But why not add some comfort to your scare? At the Ghost Theater you sit among haunted furniture and household items. Your hostess, Madame Theresa Coffin (M. T. Coffin—get it?), spins tales based on her research and experiences. Is it real? Fancy? Does it matter? Neither the Madame nor her husband, who helps run things, has a theatrical background. Nevertheless, Madame Theresa has long been intrigued by funeral homes and stories of the hereafter and she has received high marks from local reviewers. Her tales entangle audiences and leave them at times in considerable fright, if the candid pictures on her Web site are any evidence. To help keep idle hands busy, the couple also builds realistic Victorian morning clothing and other costumes, which they sell to theater groups and museums. A newly renovated performance space keeps the cutting tables out front, so visitors can appreciate all aspects of the business. There are two regularly scheduled performances: a recitation of the Madame's encounter with the spirit of the victim of a suicide (called a "psychological thriller") and a series of scary stories, all told with the lights so low that you might as well close your eyes, but don't—you never can tell when you'll have to make a sudden break for the door inches ahead of some avenging spirit. Reservations are not required for public shows, for which the box office opens fifteen minutes before the terror starts. But check ahead (508–833–1807 or www.mtcoffin.com) for the current schedule and fees, or if you want to bring a group. You don't want to be disappointed. After all, you might be dying to see it. Coffin's Ghost Theater is at 523 Main Street.

PARALLEL PARKING
Kingston

We like straight lines—they're so orderly. And what better order do they provide than when arranged as longitude and latitude, giving direction and guidance to us all? Okay, okay, so the latitude bands that run parallel to the equator and the longitude lines passing through the poles are actually big circles, and not straight at all. The point is that without them, we'd be totally lost. Those who appreciate the niceties of navigation can enjoy the pure mathematics of the way the numbers look. And one of the coolest things for the aficionados is finding a spot where either latitude or longitude is a complete whole number, with no fractions. Think of it as directional geek chic. You can enjoy a small sample of it by driving down Loring Street in Kingston, between Parks and River Streets. On the east side of the road, look for a granite slab celebrating the 42nd parallel. On that spot, you are at exactly 42 degrees latitude. Isn't it good to know where you are?

HOG WILD
Martha's Vineyard

Some motorcycle lovers says that Harley Davidsons make a deep-throated rumble that is music to their ears. It seems that the people at Panhead Mike's Offshore Cycle have taken that idea to an extreme. Sure, they tune Hogs—and totally rebuild and restore vintage bikes as well as giving attention to

the more ordinary examples. But how many cycle shops
expand into more cultural aspects of life? Panhead Mike's is
also the rehearsal space for a local band that ended up taking
its name—the Offshore Cycle Band—from its digs. And Panhead Mike's is also the official mechanic and enabler of the Flying Horses, the nation's oldest operating platform carousel. The
merry-go-round was brought from New York's Coney Island to
Oak Bluffs on the Vineyard in 1884. If you were born to be
wild, thanks to the shop, you can still take a spin from Easter
Sunday through Columbus Day and grab for the brass ring
that gives a free ride. You'll be on a hand-carved horse, but if
you'd rather try a Hog, head to the shop at 348 State Road,
Vineyard Haven or call them at (508) 693-7447. For the
carousel, go to the end of Oak Bluffs Avenue near the beach in
Oak Bluffs . . . and don't forget the leather jacket.

WHAT RELIGION HATH WROUGHT
Martha's Vineyard

We'd love to tell you when you can enjoy Illumination Night
in Oak Bluffs—really, we would. It's a warmly glittering
affair celebrating the end of summer. After a sing-along concert, the oldest member of the community lights a Japanese
lantern. Then hundreds of similar lamps are lit as they hang
on the Tabernacle, a wrought-iron open-air auditorium seating
more than 3,000. (The Tabernacle was built for religious services by the Methodists, who knew a good location for a religious revival when they saw one.) And there are even more
lanterns on the nearby gingerbread cottages. These brightly
painted wooden structures once housed those attending the
camp and are now private homes. Footpaths lead all around the
courtyards, so you can take a stroll and appreciate the colorful
dwellings in the glow.

So why don't we cough up the details of when you can see all this? It's because we don't know. The event takes place sometime in late August, but the exact date is kept a secret until about a week before it happens. You can try to pry the secret out of someone, or at least get the schedule for concerts and other activities at the Tabernacle, by calling (508) 693–0525. And if you do miss the celebration, you can still have some fun near the Tabernacle. See the cottages in the daylight or learn about the life of the early fervent inhabitants at the Cottage Museum, One Trinity Park in Oak Bluffs.

"SEA" THE BIG HORSE
Mattapoisett

If you are traveling along the main drag in Mattapoisett, an aqua-equestrian sight might leave you crying, "Whoa, Seabiscuit!" More than fifty years ago, a gift shop owner wanted something to attract attention and customers, so he asked sign maker Theodore Tetreault to build an 8-foot-tall sea horse to place on the road. And build it he did. But in the grand scheme of things, how impressive is that? The finished product was hardly taller than some professional basketball players. Once it was finished, the original owner thought that the landscape swallowed it up. So Tetreault, with the help of his two sons, went back to the stable (or was it the fishing hole?) and built a 38-foot plywood sea horse. When done, it looked almost the way it does today. (Tetreault returned later with some boat builders to add a fiberglass layer, the better to protect the steed from its native element in liquid or frozen form.) Long after the original business owner was gone, the icon stayed. After all, where does an almost 40-foot sea horse sit? Anywhere it wants.

Salty the giant sea horse has gone from kitsch to landmark.
Photo by Erik Sherman

A few years ago the sea horse came down for some rest, recreation, and rehabilitation. The decades of exposure to the elements had been hard, and eight months of work were a wonderful restorative: a new tubular frame, the removal of rotted material, fresh sherbet-colored paint, another coat of fiberglass, and a new name: Salty. Tetreault died in 2001, but his monument lives on. The land around it is now a park. How fitting: After years of working to bring in the customers, the sea horse is happily put out to literal pasture. To see it, take a drive down Route 6 by North Street.

It's a Small World
Middleborough

The lesser things in life are usually those that qualify for small talk, and these days, the public is interested in bigger and better. However, today's small was the mid-nineteenth century's big. Mercy Lavinia Warren Bump, born in Middleborough, was more—or is it less?—than diminutive. At 32 inches tall, she was one of the two most famous midgets in the country. (The other was her husband, Charles Sherwood Stratton, otherwise known as "General" Tom Thumb.) Lavinia had a sister who was also only 32 inches tall. Her other sister was normal sized, and all four of her brothers grew to over six feet. Yet she gained a level of fame that towered over that of her siblings. She spent a few years working on a relative's steam boat show on the Mississippi, then was hired by P. T. Barnum when she was 21 and dubbed "the Little Queen of Beauty." Although we're sure she was attractive, to be fair, there probably weren't a lot of contenders to the crown. Her future husband already worked for the master showman, and it would seem destiny that the two should marry, or at least form a conglomerate of their interests. Barnum turned the engagement announcement into a money-maker, putting the future bride on display for tens of thousands of people. The wedding, in 1863, was a major event in New York City, with more than 2,000 guests. The honeymooners spent time touring the world. As the years passed, both grew to 40 inches tall. After her husband's death, Lavinia lived in retirement until her marriage to Count Primo Magri, an Italian dwarf. She lived until the age of sixty-four and is buried in South Amenia, New York. But some of the personal effects of both Lavinia and Charles are on display in the Middleborough Historical Museum, which has the world's largest collection of Tom Thumb memorabilia, including his 12-inch walking stick. The collection is behind the town police station, on Jackson Street. Call ahead (508–947–1969) for the hours, though the management has been known to set up appointments at other times.

THERMOMETER MAN
Onset

What's the difference between a personal collection and a museum? Maybe just a degree of interest. Some people get all hot and bothered about a subject, but Richard Porter could be called positively mercurial—literally. He has assembled thousands of items in what he claims is the world's largest—actually, he claims that it's the world's only—thermometer museum, which sits in the basement of his home. It's also, at last check, the only museum in Onset on Cape Cod. Here are big thermometers, little thermometers, thermometers shaped like animals. There are two pill-sized thermometers that John Glenn had to swallow on his last mission on the space shuttle, which match the backup model that traveled to the moon on *Apollo 9*.

There is a thermometer that came as a prize in a Cracker Jack box, and another used in deep-sea studies. A model from Alaska reads to –100 degrees F. Some float; some are scientific instruments. Many came from flea markets and others are from Porter's travels in the United States, Europe, South America, and Africa. Porter, a retired science teacher, started his collection decades ago after a friend told him, "If you don't collect something in retirement, you may just collect dust." His teaching activities have not been left out in the cold. He regularly gives presentations at schools, museums, and conferences. You can see the collection yourself by traveling to Onset, where the museum's motto is "Always open and always free with over 3,000 to see." Call (508) 295–5504 to arrange a visit.

CABLE ENTERTAINMENT
Orleans

Sociologists and economists would argue that the telecommunications industry leaves a mark on society. We have learned that this is literally true. Just check the French Cable Station Museum, which celebrates what was a straightforward business investment of the day. Despite the reputation Yankees have of being taciturn and uncommunicative, Massachusetts became a hub of firsts in communication. Granted, this was largely because the innovators were from Europe. Alexander Graham Bell, a Scot, invented the telephone in Boston, and although the weather was against him, Italian Guglielmo Marconi looked to Cape Cod to provide a base for the first transatlantic radio broadcast—probably a good excuse to write off a vacation. But what the French Cable Museum commemorates is the time when the French, in 1869, laid their first transatlantic telegraph cable. It ran from the western tip of France to New-

The French Cable Station Museum in Orleans
celebrates the French connection.
Photo by Erik Sherman

foundland, to Orleans, and finally over to Duxbury. Given the
difficulties of ocean travel, this was an impressive engineering
feat. It was also a slow one, as the Atlantic Telegraph Company
had managed to make a transatlantic hop a few years before.
Yet being in second place didn't hinder the cable's usefulness. It
was the mechanism by which the United States learned of
Charles Lindbergh's successful landing in Paris. News from the
French end was cut off in the spring of 1940 with the message
"Les Boches sont ici—The Germans are here." The sister station
in Brest finally resumed transmission—in 1952. (We figure
that one of those famous French labor strikes might have
slowed things down after the end of the war.)

The museum is not the only legacy of the cable. To this day, you will find many Norgeots, Deschamps, and Ozons in local phone directories. These are the descendants of men who came from a French-owned set of islands near Newfoundland to work at the station. To check out the museum, go to 41 South Orleans Road, which is near the intersection of Cove Road and Route 28. It's open various hours, though not at all times of the year, so call (508) 240–1735 ahead of time to be sure.

WERE THE PILGRIMS REALLY STIFFS?
Plymouth

T he Pilgrims have a reputation for being unbending—religious, industrious, and no fun at all. Yet there is stiff, and there is . . . stiff. At the Pilgrim National Wax Museum, you can find representations of the sect that are entirely unmovable. Interest in our national forerunners is hardly unusual, and wax museums are common enough. But how many wax museums are completely devoted to the people who landed at Plymouth Rock? This one is located on Cole's Hill, where the Mayflower immigrants secretly buried their dead after their first winter on this continent so that the Wampanoag Indians would not know how their number had dwindled (amusing, as the group would have disappeared had the natives not helped them). Here, though, the dead still live. A series of dioramas show scenes of the Pilgrim's past: being jailed in England, signing the Mayflower pact, the first Thanksgiving, the blossoming love of John Alden and Priscilla Mullins. There are twenty-six scenes in all and a total of 180 figures. That's a lot of wax. If you get tired of the educational tour, then step outside, cross the street, and take in the salt air of the harbor. Just remember that this is a unique experi-

ence. In fact, you might say that no other attraction holds a
candle to it. The museum is at 15 Carver Street. You can get
more information at (508) 746–6468.

PILGRIM'S GRIND
Plymouth

L et's thank the Pilgrims for all they have done: opening a
new land to colonization, kicking out anyone who didn't
agree with their religious views, and introducing the concept
of the public utility. That's right: The next time you get angry
at the electric company, remember that you have people from
the seventeenth century to thank. When the Pilgrims almost
starved and froze to death their first year here—obviously not
having read the visitors' information—the Wampanoags taught
them to grow and store corn. But the settlers had increasing
numbers of residents to consider, and the process of grinding
corn with a mortar and pestle was either too inefficient or had
become an entirely too overwhelming drag. Enter John Jenney,
who knew that he could make use of the settlers' laziness. In
1636 he received permission to build a grinding mill, starting
a tradition of disputed charges and poor customer service that
has lasted to this day. At least reliability was there—although
the original burned down in 1847, a 1970 reconstruction
brought it back to working order; it still grinds corn, and you
can buy bags of meal. Next to it is a fish ladder, so the herring
can go upstream to spawn.

If you want to see where it all started and take a tour, head
to the corner of Leyden and Water Streets. Walk through the
park area, called Brewster Gardens; look for the small footbridge. Cross it, continue down the path along the stream, and
you will see the building at the end. Or, if you are feeling lazy,

go directly to the mill at 6 Spring Street. For more information, call (508) 747–4544, or go to www.jenneygristmill.com.
Sorry, but the complaint department isn't open today.

PLYMOUTH PEBBLE?
Plymouth

A nyone in the United States who has sat through coloring
paper turkeys at Thanksgiving has heard of Plymouth
Rock. But few know how lucky they are to see anything. First
there is the question of what the rock actually was. According
to the Pilgrim Hall Museum, none of the documents from that
time mentioned a pebble, let alone a rock. The two books of the
time written by participants said only that they had landed. It
wasn't until a hundred years later that any written works mentioned Plymouth Rock, yet somehow a local legend became
"fact." Okay; for the sake of grade school teachers everywhere
we'll be nice and say that it was the stepping stone. However,
that anything remains of the rock is a wonder. It was in the
nineteenth century that people decided to make a monument of
the rock, and the object of public affection barely survived. It
had become embedded in a wharf, and attempts to move it with
a team of oxen actually split Plymouth Rock into two pieces. So
the people took the small piece from the top and placed it
prominently in front of the town hall. At that point, all manner
of people snuck in to chip away at the stone for a souvenir. The
townsfolk decided to protect this remaining shard by carting it
off to sit behind a fence at the Pilgrim Hall Museum. Whoops—
the rock popped off the cart and cracked on the way. And at
some point, someone carved the date *1620* into the rock. (Gee,
we thought the Pilgrims found it that way.) It's just not easy
being a legend.

A local legend became fact when Plymouth Rock
was turned into a memorial.
Photo by Erik Sherman

If you visit today, you'll find Plymouth Rock behind walls and under a fancy portico on Water Street, near the end of North Street. Or you could seek out the local hotel that advertises a hot tub with a plastic replica of the big stone—a regular chip off the old granite, and maybe even as authentic.

GENDER BENDER
Provincetown

T hose with an aversion to the unusual in gender roles should avoid Provincetown in mid-October when the town hosts the Fantasia Fair, also known as TransGender week. An annual event since 1974, the Fair would more accurately be called a conference or convention. It is meant to help the transgendered live in the midst of regular society while providing "positive reinforcement and encouragement." Participants pay and register for either a half week or full week of sessions such as Daytime Makeup Tips, Trans in the Workplace, and Hormones 101. There is information for MTF (male-to-female) and FTM (female-to-male). Aside from information sessions, there are breakfasts, lunches, and dinners, and even a fashion show and musical review. This is not an occasion for gawkers, as the Fair costs a pretty penny. Those attending have paid hundreds of dollars for the full week or a discounted rate for four days and three nights, not counting lodging. Many bring partners and spouses, who pay a lower rate to take part. If you aren't part of the scene, then remember that October is past the summer season and a great time to visit a beautiful part of Cape Cod in relative quiet. Just try not to get rattled and use the wrong public restroom. For more information, see www.fantasiafair.org.

WHY? WHYDAH NOT?
Provincetown

Some people climb mountains, some swim the English Channel, and some seek shipwrecks. There is nothing else that can describe the drive that Barry Clifford has when it comes to finding boats that sank in the ocean. What can only be called an obsession of Clifford's with the pirate ship *Whydah* started when he heard stories in his youth. As an adult, he put together an expedition that had one of the great "in the nick of time" endings. After almost two years of searching, and down to his last dollar and tank of fuel, Clifford's group found the famous pirate ship, whose sunken fortunes raised Clifford's. Since then he has found the remains of one of Captain Kidd's ships, as well as a French fleet. Now Clifford thinks that he's found the *Santa Maria*—the flagship of Christopher Columbus.

At the time of this writing, there is nothing definite about the identification of Clifford's latest find, but you can visit the museum that commemorates his most famous discovery to date. The Expedition *Whydah* Sea Lab and Learning Center at 16 MacMillan Wharf features some of the 200,000 artifacts that Clifford's team brought up. Also take time to learn more about the ship, the lives of pirates, and the methods that put the jolly back in the roger. Call (508) 487–8899 or visit www.whydah .com for hours and other information.

GRUDGE GRANITE
Provincetown

T he words *Pilgrim* and *Plymouth* have a historic alliterative American accent. Yet before the *Mayflower* neared the famous P-rock, it stopped at the very end of Cape Cod, at what would eventually become P-town. (They must have been the first Provincetown summer tourists.) They even managed to sign the Mayflower Compact during their brief stop on their way to Plymouth. Not that you would know it from the way history is taught in schools. To almost everyone, the first, last, and only stop the Pilgrims made was north of the Cape. This must have left the good folks of Provincetown feeling slighted. To make sure that they got their due, the townspeople erected the Pilgrim Monument. Work began in 1907 and ended three years later.

The Pilgrim Monument is the tallest granite monument in the country, at 252 feet 7 inches. The design was copied from the Torre Del Mangia in Siena, Italy. Okay, so maybe someone was confusing the England of the Puritans with the Italy of Columbus. No matter: The view from the top can be spectacular, with Cape Cod Bay, Provincetown Harbor, and the sand dunes of the Cape Cod National Seashore visible. On a clear day, you can even see Boston. To get to that lofty sight, however, you must gain the lofty height, climbing 116 stairs and sixty ramps. After all that work, you might want to take a brief rest, which you can do in the museum while enjoying the current exhibition and remembering not to take the first Pilgrim landing spot for granite. It's not open year-round, so check http://pilgrim-monument.org or call (508) 487–1310 for information. Then drive to One High Pole Hill Road.

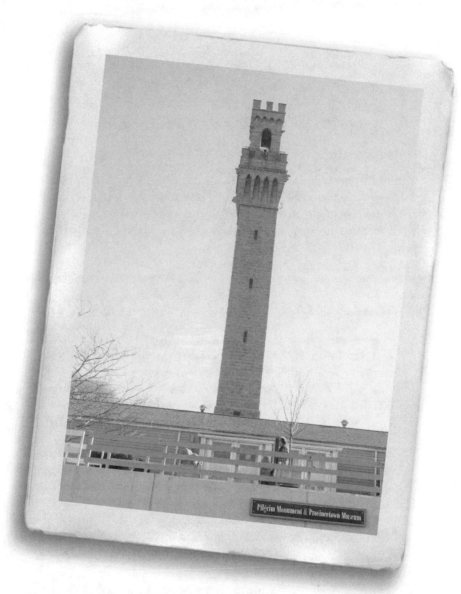

The Pilgrim Monument, the highest point in Provincetown,
celebrates the area's highest point in American history.
Photo by Erik Sherman

A Tale of Two Presidents
Quincy

L ike father, like son? There is a long tradition of offspring following parents into a line of work, except when it comes to being president of the United States. The Bushes have managed it, but before them the only case was that of John Adams

KILROY WAS IN QUINCY

A nyone whose parents lived through World War II has likely heard of Kilroy. Like an armed forces Mary and her lamb, anywhere the military went, the mysterious man was sure to go. But unlike the nursery rhyme, Kilroy was a pioneer, not a follower. Wherever GIs went, the bet was more than even money that they would find written on a wall, a monument, or even a latrine that "Kilroy was here," often accompanied by a cartoon face peering over a wall. It got to be a race among soldiers and sailors to see if they could chalk the presence in a spot before others.

What might have surprised most of those GIs was that there actually was a Kilroy: James J. Kilroy, to be exact. The man worked at the Fore River Shipyard in Quincy, once a major building facility. He was an inspector, seeing how many holes riveters would fill in a day. To avoid double-counting by some worker trying to make the job rosier, Kilroy would mark his passage by writing "Kilroy was here" with a yellow crayon. Once a and his son, John Quincy Adams. There are a number of similarities, such as both the fathers serving only one term and the sons taking office after losing the popular vote in a disputed election. But the presidents Adams were far closer, at least physically, in their origins and ends. Both were born within 75 yards of each other in the same house, and both are buried at the United First Parish in Quincy, also called the Church of the Presidents, along with their wives. The church keeps the Adams crypt open to visitors and is actually part of the Adams National Historical Park, although it receives no public funding. The rest of the park includes the birthplace of the

ship was finished and sent overseas, the expansive presence of Kilroy continued as it sailed around the world. However, no one bothered to explain the cryptic notation to the troops on the ships. Kilroy eventually got around in a big way: The name has supposedly been found on Mount Everest, the torch of the Statue of Liberty, the underside of the Arc de Triomphe, a girder on the George Washington Bridge, and in the dust on the moon. According to one probably-apocryphal story, during the Potsdam Conference, in which the United States, Great Britain, and the Soviet Union set the surrender demands for Japan, Stalin was the first to use an outhouse built for the occasion. Upon exiting, the leader reportedly turned to his aide and asked, "Who is Kilroy?" He was just this guy in Quincy. Chalk it up to a triumph of international relations. Although Kilroy is no longer there, you can see the shipyard and the United States Naval Shipbuilding Museum, which is housed on the old USS Salem, at 739 Washington Street. For information and hours, call (617) 479–7900 or visit www.uss-salem.org.

presidents as well as the Stone Library, which includes the entire book collection of John Quincy Adams. During the season, April 19 to November 10, there are guided tours of the homes. Go to the visitor center in the Galleria at Presidents Place for the first-come, first-served, first in the hearts of their—sorry, wrong president—tours. There is validated parking and a free trolley between the center and the historic homes about every thirty minutes on the quarter hour. For more information, call (617) 770–1175 or visit www.nps.gov/adam.

WILL THE REAL PETER PLEASE HOP UP?
Sandwich

K now the name Thornton W. Burgess? This native of Sandwich may not sound familiar, but chances are that you know some of his creations: Peter Rabbit, Hooty Owl, Grandfather Skunk, and Jimmy Skunk. Naturalist and author Burgess wrote more than 170 books and some 15,000 stories—enough to keep a child out of trouble for at least part of the formative years. Now you too can avoid some trouble in two facilities: a museum and a nature center.

The Thornton W. Burgess Society runs a museum in a house once owned by Burgess's Aunt Arabella. It is filled with memorabilia, art, and other items of interest; an herb garden and pond are out back. (There is a nominal entrance fee during the open season of April through October.)

Yet while looking into the museum's history, we ran into a bit of a problem. One Burgess character was Peter Rabbit, as his books and the Society Web site show. Yet there is a different Peter Rabbit, written by author and animal lover Beatrix Potter. According to a bit of online snooping, it seems that Potter's first book, *The Tale of Peter Rabbit,* appeared in 1902. The Burgess Peter Rabbit was in part of a set of syndicated children's stories illustrated by Harrison Cady, which appeared in 1910 as newspaper columns. So the timing is close, but the two characters are different in age and temperament, and the two authors were separated by the Atlantic Ocean. We guess that Peter is a common enough name, even among rabbits.

One difference between the two animal worlds is that Burgess's Peter Rabbit lived in a briar patch. If the kids, or the kid-in-you, want to move around more, wander over to the Green Briar Nature Center, open all year and situated next to a briar patch— yes, the one in the stories. You can find workshops, natural history programs, and some pleasant walking trails in a fifty-seven-acre conservation area, all open to the public. And while you're there, take a peek into the Green Briar Jam Kitchen. Call ahead, and you may be able to catch a jam-making workshop. The Robert S. Swain Natural History Library, containing books, magazines, and other materials on the flora and fauna of the Northeast, rounds out the visit. For more information, visit the museum at 4 Water Street (Route 130; 508–888–4668) or the Green Briar Nature Center and Jam Kitchen, 6 Discovery Hill Road in East Sandwich (508–888-6870).

CORN HILL
Truro

Pilgrims? Plymouth Rock. It's a match made in the history books. But that town wasn't the ship's only stopping place. Right before landing there, the immigrants stopped on Cape Cod in the areas that would become Eastham, Provincetown, and Truro. After making some sojourns for supplies and a break for washing clothes—inspiring, we are sure, the

REVOLUTIONARY
FEMINIST FIGHTER

When we hear the phrase "daughters of the American revolution," the images that come to mind include petticoats, churning butter by hand, sewing clothes, and picking up the eggs for breakfast from under the hens. But Deborah Samson, descended from Gov. William Bradford of Mayflower fame, would tend to wearing trousers, shooting guns, and fighting. Blame it on poverty and a father who abandoned her, but this was a woman who could take care of herself. This native of Plympton also became the first woman to masquerade as a man and fight in the Revolutionary War.

Samson's father went to sea and her mother couldn't make ends meet, so Samson lived with relatives and, at age ten, became an indentured servant to a family of ten. She stayed in this position until she was eighteen. Hard labor developed her strength and she learned to shoot a musket as well as to spin, weave, and cook. In other words, this was a woman to be reckoned with. When two of the sons of the family that she lived with were killed, her fate was decided.

Samson borrowed clothes from a man named Samuel Leonard, disguised herself as a boy called Timothy Thayer, and joined the Continental Army. Then in 1782, at age twenty-one, she enlisted in the Fourth Massachusetts Regiment under the name of Robert Shurtleff. She was 5 foot 7 inches tall and she bound her breasts to look like a lad. Other soldiers assumed that "Robert" was too young to have started shaving. Good thing they didn't check her legs. Eventually an illness revealed the truth, and she had her honorable discharge personally handed to her by George Washington. Obviously he knew better than to make her mad.

Samson even received a pension eventually, thanks to the intercession of Paul Revere, and her husband was granted a widow's pension after her death at age sixty-six, to complete the tale of gender reversal. In 1983 she was named the official heroine of Massachusetts. A plaque honoring Samson is on the Plympton Town Green; go to 11 North Main Street in Sharon to see a statue of her.

Corn Hill was once the site of perfidious provisions pilfering.
Photo by Erik Sherman

Laundromat—a group of men went exploring. While tromping about, they stumbled upon some fields cleared for farming and a store of corn, as well as a metal kettle that looked as though it came from Europe. After taking as much corn as they could carry to plant later, they buried the rest in the kettle. We can hear the conversation now: "Jumping Jehoshaphat, Brother Ephraim, look at all this corn. Good thing there's nobody here that it belongs to. Let's scram." That corn was a literal life saver; roughly ten bushels provided a crop for the spring and a welcome source of food after a winter that would kill a frighteningly large percentage of the party. So the successful colonization of Massachusetts started with an act of larceny. Good thing there were no laws making it illegal.

The Pilgrims vowed to make restitution, having a sneaking suspicion that the corn belonged to someone. Eventually they put two and two together and realized that it was Indian corn. The restitution came in the form of the weeklong feast that we now commemorate as Thanksgiving (to say nothing of disease, war, and land-grabbing). You can see the historic spot, called Corn Hill, and a commemorative marker near Corn Hill Road off Route 6, which is a darned sight harder to find than the corn was. While you are there, enjoy the beach.

TOWERING TALENT
Truro

E very age has its superstars. Even before music videos, CDs, and movies, there were performers who could command enthusiastic mayhem. One of them was Jenny Lind, the soprano known as the "Swedish Nightingale." She started playing piano at age four and eventually attended the Royal Theater School to study music, dance, and acting. She had her first big opera role at age seventeen, and she soon became the leading singer in Europe. Taking into account the slower pace of communications and travel, it is difficult to appreciate the furor that could bubble up about Lind's performances. When she came to New York for a concert tour promoted by showman P. T. Barnum, nearly 40,000 suckers . . . ah, adoring fans . . . lured by the masterful publicity packed the docks to welcome her arrival by ship.

As part of her tour, Lind was scheduled to sing in Boston in 1850, but someone massively oversold the concert and many of the people who paid their money could not fit in the building. According to legend, which seems to be unsupported by newspaper accounts at the time, Lind climbed to the top of

*The Jenny Lind Tower is visible from the
Highland Light Beach parking area.*
Photo by Erik Sherman

an adjoining 55-foot tower to sing to the people in the street.
Perhaps another piece of Barnum's hokum? Could be. However, in 1927, the tower was slated for demolition. Harry M.
Aldrich, supposedly a serious Jenny Lind fan, bought the
structure. He had it moved, stone by stone, to North Truro by
train, and then by horse-drawn cart to its present location in
Truro. The building, which came to be known as the Jenny
Lind Tower, was deeded in 1961 to the Cape Cod National
Seashore by Aldrich's daughter-in-law. You can't get to the
tower without trespassing on private land, but you can drive
up Highland Road and park at the Highland Light Beach
parking lot to take a look and a bow.

A PLACE MADE FOR RADIO
Wellfleet

Guglielmo Marconi was the first person to make it big in radio. First he invented it; then he demonstrated the first transatlantic broadcast in 1901. Too bad that he couldn't have staged his demonstration in Wellfleet, and moved to Canada instead.

Cape Cod was Marconi's preferred location, and his team was erecting transmission equipment there in 1901. Unfortunately, the quality of construction left something to be desired. In August, just two months after building had started, a stiff breeze bent the heads of the antenna mast and the Italian inventor moved north, where men were men and radio towers were sturdy. It was the first case of cheaply made electronics equipment with no written warranty in sight. So much for history.

In the fall of 1901, the masts totally collapsed. It wouldn't be until January 18, 1903 that the station finally was put back into commission. A transmission occurred from the United States, with Pres. Theodore Roosevelt sending a message to King Edward VII of England. The Wellfleet station remained in operation until the U.S. Navy closed it in 1917 for safety reasons. (How surprising.) The area became a military camp and, eventually, part of the Cape Cod National Seashore. Today some tower footings and a bit of the station's foundation are all that is left. There is an informative display as well as a pleasant beach, which is good because you will probably tire of the placards even faster than the towers fell. Head over to Marconi Site Road and drive down, following the signs to the beach. For more information, call (508) 255–3421.

BELLY CONFUSING
Wellfleet

T he Wellfleet town clock confuses the uninitiated. When its
bell rings four times, it is 6:00 in the morning . . . unless it
is 10:00 A.M., 2:00 P.M., or the middle of the night. No, the
mechanism is not broken. Wellfleet has the only town clock
that rings on ship's time. It's a complex system in which the
day is broken into watches and then subdivided into hours
marked by anywhere from one to eight bells.

The story of how the
clock ended up here
is happily simpler. It
was the brainchild of
a town selectman in
1952, Lawrence Gar-
dinier, who was a bril-
liant tinkerer without
a formal education.
Because of the mar-
itime history of the
area, he wanted a town
ship's clock. After con-
vincing others to go
along with the idea,

The First Congregational Church
in Wellfleet is believed to have
the only town clock that rings on
ship's time.
Photo by Erik Sherman

Gardinier proposed a budget of $500 to create a striking mechanism for the three-faced clock in the steeple of the First Congregational Church, which was just ornamental. Combining motors, relays, wire, mechanisms, and other bells and whistles, he rigged a device that would ring the church bell the proper number of times at the correct hours. His contraption was used for twenty years before it was replaced for the most part by an electronic system. However, on special occasions, the old bell system still delivers on time, every time. You can see and hear the time at 200 Main Street.

LETTING THE CHIPS FALL
Whitman

Most roads lead somewhere, and most signs are put in place to draw attention to something. But there is the odd dead end and at least one carefully tended sign advertising a business that has been gone since the mid-1980s.

The story of the phantom sign has a uniquely sweet beginning. Most cookies don't have the prominence to deserve a history. Not so the original chocolate chip cookie—the toll house—which really came about by accident. Kenneth and Ruth Wakefield ran the Toll House Inn in Whitman. The building had originally been a toll booth on the road between New Bedford and Boston. One day in 1930 Ruth was baking a batch of cookies for customers. She usually chopped up baker's chocolate for this particular recipe, and the dark chunks would melt into the dough. One day she ran out of her usual ingredient and instead turned to the next chocolate thing she had: a bar of Nestlé semi-sweet. But instead of melting in, the bits of chocolate kept their shape. The cookie became a hit, her recipe

Pay no attention to the pointing hand. You can't
get there from here.
Photo by Erik Sherman

was published in some newspapers, and sales for the chocolate
bar went through the roof. Ruth then approached Nestlé. She
struck a deal with the company, and the recipe appeared on the
candy bar wrapping. Sales continued to improve and the company eventually started scoring the bar and including a special
chopper. In 1939 Nestlé finally created a bag of special chocolate pieces that worked well in the recipe, and smart business
met culinary history.

The Toll House Inn went through several owners and
finally burned down on New Year's Eve in 1984. Ruth Wakefield died in 1977 and is buried in the Mayflower Cemetery at
774 Tremont Street (Route 3A) in Duxbury. However, you
might call the one remnant of the late Toll House Inn the marketing equivalent of a headstone. To this day, if you go to
Route 18, right near the intersection of Route 14, standing
proudly between two fast-food emporiums is the sign.

GOLF GRAVE
Yarmouth Port

We come into the world alone and we leave alone—unless we
have company. Many old graveyards in Massachusetts are
filled with figures from politics, literature, and the arts. They
tend to be crowded, as free space is scarce. But in Yarmouth
Port on Cape Cod, there is a singular phenomenon: a cemetery
with a single gravestone sitting on a golf course. In December
1801, a sixty-four-year-old resident, John Hall, died. The cause
of his death was smallpox, which, although long controlled
now, was a scourge of the world at that time. It was contagious
and a killer. In those days, people figured that the safest thing
was to keep everyone, and every corpse, with the disease far
away from the uninfected. And so, John Hall had a solitary
grave in the woods, as happened in other towns on the Cape.

Eventually, someone decided to build the Kings Way Golf
Club in that same patch of woods. In clearing the trees, they
found Hall's final resting place. It was neither a natural hazard
nor something that could be moved, so it became part of the
scene. Was John Hall married, and if so, can we call the Widow
Hall the first literal golf widow in this country?

Protecting the grave is a low, heavy chain supported by

John Hall's compact abode rests behind a sand trap.
Photo by Erik Sherman

short pillars. We assume that should a ball stray onto the grave, it must be considered dead, with the player losing a stroke. Here's hoping that Mr. Hall continues to find peace— and maybe a mulligan or two. To pay your respects to the late Mr. Hall, and to any wayward golf balls, go to the course by taking King's Circuit off Route 6A. Follow the large circular drive around the course, look for the sign that says "13," take the side street, and look for the parking area on the right. The grave is past the trees, on the right-hand side of the green for the par-three hole.

CENTRAL MASSACHUSETTS

CENTRAL
MASSACHUSETTS

. . . S E V E N ,   S I X ,   F I V E ,   F O R E !

A u b u r n

H alfway between the tee and the green on the ninth fairway
of the Pakachoag Golf Course in the town of Auburn is a
unique hazard: a stone marker commemorating the flight of
the first successfully launched liquid-fueled rocket. Robert Goddard, a physics professor at nearby Worcester Polytechnic
Institute, set off his 10-foot rocket on March 16, 1926, on what
was then his aunt's farm. Goddard's gas- and liquid-oxygen
powered missile, nicknamed "Nell," soared 41 feet into the
heavens before landing in a frozen cabbage patch. The hometown newspaper's headline the next day read: "Moon rocket
misses target by 238,799½ miles."

The successful, if not stratosphere-breaking, launch earned
Goddard the title the "Father of Modern Rocketry," and today
road signs leading into Worcester proudly honor the hometown
scientist. Quite a different reception from the one the *New
York Times* gave Goddard in 1929. The prestigious newspaper
proclaimed him a crackpot who lacked "the knowledge ladled
out daily in high schools." Everyone knew, reported the *Times,*
that space travel as theorized by Goddard was impossible
because without atmosphere to push against, a rocket could
not move. Despite Goddard's certainty that Newton's law of
action and reaction was with him, the article sent the scientist

into a funk from which, despite his aeronautical achievements, he never really did recover. In 1969, after the first lunar landing, the *New York Times* published a correction.

Long after his death in 1945, Goddard posthumously received scores of honors, including the Congressional Medal and the National Inventors Hall of Fame Award. The awards are part of the extensive collection of Goddard memorabilia in the Goddard Library at Clark University. A time capsule containing a replica of a rocket Goddard built in 1940 and some dirt from his aunt's farm launch site is encased in concrete in the floor leading to the library. The rocket–time capsule is to be opened in 2466, five hundred years after it was dedicated by Vice Pres. Hubert Humphrey.

WORLD'S BIGGEST GARAGE SALE
Brimfield

Are you an inveterate collector? Is that being kind? Do friends and family more often use the term "pack rat"? If so, you will be in rat . . . uh, hog heaven three times a year at the Brimfield Fair. The fair is the work of a number of event producers, all of whom have their own staked-out spots. On a Tuesday through Sunday in late spring, summer, and early fall, 5,000 or more antiques dealers from all over the country converge here, lining a mile of Route 20. Add bargain-hunting crowds and you have something modern in the midst of the old treasures—a traffic jam.

Planning an outing through Brimfield on a show day is something like planning the Normandy invasion. If you are a serious shopper, do not—we repeat, do *not*—decide to "wing it."

Go to www.brimfield.com and check out the pre-show schedule. Also, come prepared. You'll want a backpack to carry your swag. And, another must, don't claim to be with the Internal Revenue Service; cash is by far the preferred currency. Another piece of advice: these dealers have paid good money to attend, and show organizers aren't inclined to offer refunds, no matter what the weather, so if it rains, quickly find an umbrella. Don't put off a trip until the last hours, as dealers often wrap up early. If you're so inclined, it's okay to buy some new things while you are there; they'll probably be antiques by the time you finally get out of traffic.

YOU SAY IT YOUR WAY, I'LL SAY IT MINE
Dudley

L ake Webster, in the town of Dudley, is also known as Lake Chargoggagoggmanchauggagoggchaubunagungamaugg. And contrary to popular opinion, the lake with the longest name in the United States does not mean "You fish on your side, I fish on my side, nobody fishes in the middle." The real meaning of the elongated word is derived from the local Indian name that means "Englishmen at Manchaug at the fishing place at the boundary." The Englishman in this particular instance was one Samuel Slater, who built a mill near the lake, near the village where the Monuhchogok Indians lived.

Lake Chargoggagoggmanchauggagoggchaubunagunga-maugg is more than 1,400 acres in size and composed of three lakes joined by narrow channels. You'll probably find wide-mouth bass there. Very wide-mouth bass.

SIT DOWN AND BE COUNTED
Gardner

They've been making chairs in Gardner since 1805. By 1837 they were turning out so many chairs that residents immodestly dubbed the place "Chair City of the World." Then in 1905 the town commemorated the one-hundredth anniversary of its chairmaking industry by building a 12-foot-tall mission chair. But the folks in Thomasville, North Carolina, the self-proclaimed "Furniture and Hosiery Capital of the World," weren't about to take a back seat to Gardner. So in 1928 they built a chair that was a foot and a half taller.

Over the next seventy-five years, other cities built increasingly larger chairs to lay claim to the throne as the king of chairdom. In Bennington, Vermont, they built a 19-foot 1-inch-tall ladderback. Again, Thomasville wasn't about to take this sitting down. They built a chair 5 inches taller. Morristown, Tennessee, got into the fray with a 20-foot-tall green sheet metal recliner. Then in 1976, for the bicentennial, Gardner defended the north's honor by building a 20-foot 7-inch-high job. The local Rotary Club in Gardner commissioned Leon W. Plante to design the mother of all chairs. His creation, 10 feet wide and 9 feet deep, stands (or sits, as the case may be) in front of the Helen Mae Sauter Elementary School at 130 Elm Street. However, Gardner sat tall in the saddle for just a year, when its chair was upstaged by a 24-foot 9-inch tall ladderback in Binghamton, New York.

In June 2002 rustic furniture maker Bim Willow of Michigan bent branches into a behemoth 55-footer and says he will build a 70-foot willow tree chair on request. It's left the competition weeping.

While you are in Gardner, you'll also see a 15-foot pretender to the throne on Route 2A.

*It may not be the largest chair in the world, but
Gardner's 20-foot 7-inch model is the biggest in
the Bay State.*
Photo courtesy of Yulia Govorushko

YE WITH LITTLE FAITH, THE WOR-SHIP

Hudson

Apparently the Rev. Louis Winthrop West was bored with
retirement and wanted to do a little ministering. So in the
summer of 1953, he began constructing a church on the front
lawn of his house on Central Street in Hudson. By September
he had put the finishing touches on his house of worship. It
didn't take long to build because it wasn't very big. In fact, Reverend West's Union Church of All Faiths was the smallest
church in the world. The mini-sanctuary measured just 5 feet
wide, 11 feet deep, and 10 feet high. Inside, on the back wall, a
20-square-foot painting depicted a sailing ship grounded on
rocks. Its title: *In the Cross of Christ I Glory*. The nautical
theme was continued atop the church, where the steeple
housed a bell from a Coast Guard vessel. Reverend West also
placed a golf ball under the church's mini-weather vane.

Over the years more than 10,000 people have signed the
tiny church's guest books. More than 600 weddings have taken
place in the petite structure. Obviously Reverend West thought
small was beautiful, because a few years later he built an even
smaller church, measuring just 5 feet by 9 and a half feet at
his summer home in Wiscasset, Maine. It was later dismantled.

When Reverend West died in 1966, his son, Horace, took
over the micro-nondenominational church. The church was
open 24/7 year-round until vandals broke two crosses and left
beer bottles on the floor. Then in the fall of 1977, the tiny
chapel was moved down the street to the rear of the First Fed-
erated Church, where it was rededicated but little used. Eventually the steeple fell off.

Vic Petkauskos, a contractor from Hyannis who grew up in
Hudson in the 1950s, always remembered passing Reverend
West's tiny church. In the spring of 2003, Petkauskos bought

The smallest church in the world was built by
Rev. Louis Winthrop West in Hudson.
Photo courtesy of the Hudson Historical Society

what remained of the building, hauled it to his garage on Cape
Cod, and began repairing "the whole shooting match." He
installed a new floor and even built a new steeple with stained-
glass windows. Petkauskos plans to place the church on a
barge, decorate it with flowers, and hold weddings afloat off
the coast of the Cape. The little church that could, still can.

THE SUNNY SIDE UP
Leominster

For years a giant frying pan that weighs 380 pounds, is 9 feet in diameter, and has an 8-foot-long handle, hung on the outside of Rob's Country Kitchen at 23 Sack Boulevard. Obviously, Rob couldn't stand the heat because in April 2004 he got out of the kitchen . . . and the restaurant biz. Today you will find Al Dente Pizzeria at the address. The giant pan still hangs outside, but now it holds several slices of very large pizza.

FEATHERSTONE'S FLAMINGOS
Leominster

Florida may have the real thing, but Massachusetts has the biggest flock of fake flamingos in the United States. Leominster is home to the plastic pink variety that have been produced by Union Products since 1957. The feather in the cap for the idea goes to Don Featherstone, who created the classic lawn ornament soon after he started working at the company. (His first design for the firm was an anatomically correct duck, but it didn't fly.) However, sales of the flightless 3-foot-tall birds immediately took off; more than 20 million of the Pepto-Bismol-colored birds have been sold.

In 1986 Featherstone's signature was added to the statue to guarantee authenticity, but when he retired from Union Products in 2000, the company removed his John Hancock. Traditionalists flocked together and caused quite a flap when they

Don and Nancy Featherstone hold
flightless fancy birds of his design.
Photo by Bruce Gellerman

heard the news, calling for a boycott against buying the statues sans his signature.

In the summer, to commemorate the year Featherstone created his first plastic fine-feathered friend, he and his wife,
Nancy, place fifty-seven of the birds in their cement-covered
backyard. In the winter they install a pair of "snomingos"
(albino models of the birds).

Nancy and Don are a strange pair of birds themselves.
Every day for the past twenty-six years, they have worn identi-
cal outfits she sews. Two years prior to that, before they were
married, they wore the same outfits only on weekends.

SAY HELLO TO SOMEONE IN MASSACHUSETTS

Lenny Gomulka is no Lawrence Welk, but he has penned a high-stepping polka worthy of the bubble master himself. His tune, "Say Hello to Someone in Massachusetts," is the official polka of the commonwealth. Lenny wrote the catchy little ditty in a moment of inspiration. He was driving near his home in Ludlow when the tune just came to him. He grabbed his handheld tape recorder and thankfully preserved the polka for posterity.

Despite the fact that it is really, really hard to come up with words that rhyme with Massachusetts, *the state has more than its fair share of official songs. Arlo Guthrie's "Massachusetts" is the official state folk song. "The Road to Boston" is the official ceremonial march. The official patriotic song is "The Great State of Massachusetts," and let's not forget the official state ode, appropriately titled, "Ode to Massachusetts."*

While we're on the subject, Massachusetts has a penchant for making things official. The cranberry, for example, is twice blessed. It's the state berry and the official beverage.

Johnny Appleseed of Leominster is the state folk hero, and Deborah Samson is the state heroine. (Samson dressed as a man and went by the name Robert Shurtleff *to fight in the Revolutionary War.) The Boston terrier is the official bowser, the tabby is the official state cat, Boston cream pie (which is actually a cake) is the official dessert, and the titmouse is the official state bird. And, in case you were wondering, the ladybug became the state insect in 1974 after intense lobbying of the legislature by second-graders from Franklin, Massachusetts.*

S Y N (T H E T I C)   C I T Y ,   U S A
L e o m i n s t e r

ifteen years before Dustin Hoffman received unsolicited
career advice in the 1967 movie *The Graduate,* Brownie Wise
was cleaning up in plastics. Brownie Wise was a marketing
genius who built an empire out of bowls that burped. Wise
teamed up with Earl Silas Tupper, the inventor of the bowls that
bear his name, and their work earned them a place in plastics
history. Today a Tupperware party is held somewhere in the
world every two and a half seconds, and 90 percent of American
homes own at least one piece of the flexible containers.

The story of Tupperware is just one of the plastic fantastic
tales told at the National Plastics Center and Museum in
Leominster. From bulletproof "glass" and Styrofoam cups to
Saran wrap and soda bottles, the past, present, and future of
plastics is presented at the museum.

The museum that pays homage to plastics and polymers is
aptly placed. In Leominster nearly half the companies are
involved in the plastics industry. You could say the pioneering
plastic city got its roots as the comb capital of the world. In
1770 Obidiah Hill moved to Leominster and began making
combs by hand out of natural materials. By 1885 there were
twenty-five comb companies in the city. As the demand
increased and the supply of horn, tortoise shell, and ivory
became scarce, the hunt for a replacement material began. A
hundred years later, when celluloid (the first semi-synthetic
material) was developed, one of its first uses was in making
combs. Unfortunately, celluloid was highly flammable. For the
next thirty years it caused many a bad hair day, until a safer
plastic was invented.

Among those honored in the museum's Plastic Hall of Fame
are John Wesley Hyatt, "the grandfather of plastics," and Roy

Plunkett, the inventor of Teflon. But you won't find Dustin Hoffman among the notables, even though he has made his career in celluloid. Inexplicably, another notable exclusion to the Plastic Hall of Fame is Don Featherstone, creator of the pink plastic flamingo.

The National Plastics Center and Museum is located on Derwin Street off Route 117. For the museum's hours of operation, call (978) 537-9529 or visit: www.plasticsmuseum.org/home .html.

A TOWERING ACCOMPLISHMENT, IN A ROUNDABOUT WAY
Milford

We've heard of keeping those native traditions when you travel, but this seems extreme. Ireland has round towers scattered about, erected at the time that the Vikings—the Scandinavian raiders, not the fancy kitchen stoves—were looting the coast of western Europe. To the Irish, the Vikings were technical wizards, with fast ships and tempered-steel swords, who also had an advantage with a degree of organization not available to the separate European tribes. They were also wizards at pillaging and burning. The latter was particularly problematic when what went into the fire were priceless illuminated manuscripts, often the only copy of works of learning. Dealing with the Dark Ages was bad enough, and no one likes to start over, especially when the job takes months, so the Irish monks responsible for the manuscripts began to build round towers, nearing 100 feet in height, with doors some 15 feet off the ground. When the Vikings came a-callin', they had a hard time a-knockin': The community would climb a rope ladder into the tower to seek refuge, then pull the ladder up behind them. A lookout floor at the tower's top allowed them to see when things were clear and they could leave. It was frustrating for the invading hordes and a relief to the monks, who must have figured that the privations of the early monastic life were ample hardship. Of the original one hundred towers, sixty-five still survive in Ireland. And a single one remains in North America, at St. Mary of the Assumption Cemetery (27 Pearl Street, Milford). It's shorter than its native brethren, rising only 65 feet. The cemetery, one of the first Catholic burial grounds in Massachusetts, was built around the turn of the twentieth century by Irish immigrant stone workers who decided to re-create one of the structures from their mother-land. They must have had a tough time leaving work at the office. Did anyone tell them that while the Vikings did come to America, it was eight hundred or nine hundred years earlier?

NOWHERESVILLE, USA
Podunk

Yes, Virginia, there is a Podunk. The place, whose name is usually analogous with Nowheresville, is an unincorporated town of about 6 square miles located in East Brookfield, about 15 miles west of Worcester. About a hundred families live there. *Podunk* is the Indian word for bog or swamp. And this town is podunky.

The town includes the Podunk Gift Barn and the Podunk Cemetery. To visit Podunk, permanently or otherwise, from Route 9/West Main Street in East Brookfield (hey, we said it was Nowheresville), travel south on Philip Quinn Memorial Highway. The road turns into Podunk Pike. Where the Pike intersects Adams Street and Adams Road, just before the cemetery, a sign welcomes you to Podunk.

THE ONE AND ONLY EWE
Sterling and Sudbury

For the past two centuries, the towns of Sterling, Massachusetts, and Newport, New Hampshire, have been locking horns over a critical civic matter. Did Mary really have a little lamb, or are she and her mutton just a myth? At stake in the historic debate is a claim to fame, if not fortune.

Sterling says that in 1815, when Mary Sawyer Tyler lived in the town, she had a little lamb named Nathaniel and it did indeed follow her to school one day. A visitor from Harvard University reportedly witnessed the entire event and penned the poem.

Supporting Sterling's version of things are reports that seventy-three years later Ms. Tyler announced that she was *the* Mary. She used her fame to solicit donations to restore Boston's Old South Meeting House by selling wool from unraveled socks made from *the* lamb's fleece.

You can find a statue of the scholarly Nathaniel in the Sterling town square. There is also an entire room in the town's historical society dedicated to his memorable trip to school. Descendants of Ms. Mary Sawyer Tyler still dress up as Mary, and her lamb dutifully follows in the town's annual parade.

Folks 70 miles away in Newport, New Hampshire, say they have evidence that makes mincemeat out of Sterling's claim to Mary's fame. They say there was no Mary, no lamb, and no school. It seems that Newport poet and abolitionist Mary Hale made up the entire thing and published the catchy little ditty in 1830. Newport's claim is supported by the *Oxford Book of Nursery Rhymes,* which lists Hale as the author but notes the historical controversy.

To complicate the lamb's tale, the little red schoolhouse to which Mary allegedly went is in Sudbury, Massachusetts, not

The lamb statue in Sterling.
Photo by Bruce Gellerman

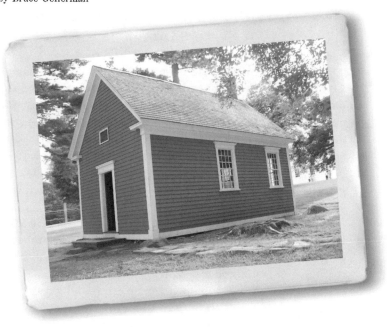

The red schoolhouse in Sudbury.
Photo by Bruce Gellerman

Sterling. Reportedly, Henry Ford discovered a barn built out of wood from the original school in Sterling, had it disassembled, and then rebuilt the one-room schoolhouse in Sudbury. Ewe figure it out.

A statue of Nathaniel, the lamb whose fleece was white as snow, can be found in Sterling's town square on Route 62.

The Little Red School House in Sudbury is located on Wayside Inn Road off Route 20 South. It's open from May 15 to October 15, Wednesday through Sunday, 11:30 A.M. to 5:00 P.M. But to make sure school is in session and you're not tardy, call (978) 443–1776.

YES, HELL DOES FREEZE OVER
Sutton

Purgatory Chasm State Reservation, in the southeastern part of central Massachusetts, is an immense, unique, and perplexing place. Nearly half a mile long and fifty feet wide, its perpendicular walls rise 70 feet high in some places. Scientists are at a loss to explain how the chasm was formed. Some believe it was created 14,000 years ago when an earth dam holding back melted glacial ice suddenly burst and eroded the granite rock. Others suggest it was formed only a few hundred years ago by an earthquake.

Whatever the cause, the area now offers a lot of hiking trails, places to climb, and caves, along with a number of interesting rock formations bearing quirky names such as the Coffin, Lover's Leap, and Fat Man's Misery.

Purgatory Chasm is open year-round, and good hiking shoes are a must, especially in the winter. Purgatory freezes over and the rocks are very slippery. For more information call Purgatory Chasm State Reservation at (508) 234–3733.

From the Mass Pike (Interstate 90), take exit 10A to Route
146 South and follow the signs to Purgatory Road.

His Name Is Danger—At Least, We Think It Is
Wales

There is a category of words called *eponyms*—that's when
people's names convey their occupations or environmental
conditions, such as Dr. Cutter, the surgeon, or a fisherman
named Baiter. We don't know if Doug Danger is the name this
daredevil was born with, but if the shoe fits, throw it over
dozens of cars. Danger did this literally, all the while keeping
his foot in the shoe. In 1990 he sent his motorcycle soaring
and cleared either forty-two cars, parked side-by-side, for a
total of 251 feet, or thirty-eight cars, depending on who is
recounting the record. Either way, that's longer than the
efforts of the more famous Evel Knievel.

You might think that a modicum of fame would satisfy
someone, but apparently *danger* in some language translates to
"insane undertaking." Some riders have actually died trying
to break this record. Danger is still alive, but that is due only
to luck and competent medical care. The year after setting the
record, he missed an eleven-car jump and crashed, breaking
seventeen bones and winding up in a month-long coma.

For most people, that would have been a sign to hang up
the leather chaps. But unfortunately for Danger, he had complete memory loss as a result of an accompanying head injury,
so even if he had learned a lesson, he forgot it. The man actually returned to jumping motorcycles, even though, as his own
Web site (www.dougdanger.net) states, he had little memory of
anything, including how to jump a motorcycle. Danger is a

fast learner, though, because he has since managed to jump
seventeen semi-trucks as well as an L–1011 jumbo jet, wing tip
to wing tip. Hopefully it was on the ground at the time.

A FLY-BY-WEEKEND MUSEUM
Winchendon

T he Top Fun Aviation Toy Museum is all about the Wright
stuff. It is the only museum in the world devoted to
aviation-related toys. Its mission is to "give children's dreams
the Wright wings." Here, on the first floor of the Old Murdock
School, kids will find noteworthy (if not airworthy) toys, from
hot air balloons to space craft. There are flying toys from
around the world made with metal, plastic, and wood. There
are cast-iron statues of Bugs Bunny in his plane, and Olive Oyl
soars in a die-cast model. A helicopter and an airplane made by
children in Burkina Faso were fashioned from Dutch milk tins.
Covering the entire wall of one room is an "On-the-Wall Airport" offering a pilot's-eye view of the ground and the feeling
that you're flying overhead.

The museum encourages kids to take flights of fantasy and
test-fly their balsa and paper creations in the large, high-
ceiling activity room. The Top Fun Aviation Toy Museum is at
22 Murdock Avenue, about an hour west of Boston as the crow
flies. If you feel like winging it, the closest airport is in Gardner. For hours and directions, call (978) 297–4337 or visit
www.topfunaviation.com/default.htm.

WATCH IT WITH THAT FORK, BUSTER!
Worcester

In August business is slow at the Sole Proprietor in Worcester. So to inflate sales the proprietor of the seafood restaurant calls upon Buster the Crab to pump up the volume. Buster is the world's largest inflatable crab. He has a 75-foot claw span and, if he were real, he'd feed 200,000 people. Of course, according to his owners, that would require 35,116 pounds of butter, 45,447 lemons, and who-knows-how-many moist towelettes.

The Sole Proprietor is at 118 Highland Avenue, (508) 798–FISH. Tell 'em Buster sent you.

Buster the Crab presides over his favorite Worcester restaurant every August. Photo by Bruce Gellerman

SECOND FIRSTS

In the 1970s Worcester residents affectionately began calling their city "Wormtown" because it was, well, lifeless and it spoofed Boston's "Beantown." More recently local boosters have started calling Worcester "the Paris of the 00s." While we wouldn't necessarily go that far, being the second largest city in Massachusetts (and in New England) does not mean that Worcester is an also-ran. Far from it.

According to administrators at the Hampton Inn in downtown Worcester, "the city is the center of the known universe." Notwithstanding Beantown's claim to that title, each of the hotel's five stories is a unique tribute to the second city's many firsts, featuring books, memorabilia, and photographs. The hotel employees have also been schooled in Worcester lore and are brimming with facts and figures.

Consider these noteworthy Worcester claims to fame:

- *WORC–AM disc jockey Dick "the Derby" Smith was the first DJ to play a Beatles song in the United States. The grateful Fab Four gave him a gold record of "She Loves You" and signed it, "To the first true believer."*

- *America's first Nobel Prize went to Albert A. Michelson of Clark University (in 1902, for his measurement of light).*

- *In 1952 Frank A. Firoillo was the first to market a pizza pie mix; five years earlier he had the first pizza stand in Worcester.*

- *The monkey wrench was invented in Worcester in 1840 by Loring and Aury Coes of the Coes Knife Company.*

- *Albert Tolman of Worcester built a "man-drawn lorry" for a missionary heading to South America in 1846. The rickshaw was an instant hit in Asia.*

- *Worcester was once "the shredded wheat capital of the world." Henry Perky of Worcester created the flaky breakfast biscuit in his Jackson Street factory.*

- *In 1833 Worcester State Hospital became the nation's first publicly financed insane asylum. That same year the Boston and West Worcester Rail Road became the first in the country to charge commuter fares.*

- *The first typewriter and ballpoint pen were both invented in Worcester.*

- *Last but not least, Worcester was the second city to celebrate First Night. (Boston was the first.)*

The Poop on Indoor Plumbing
Worcester

The curators of the American Sanitary Plumbing Museum have been the butt of countless jokes, so don't even try to pull their chain. Despite the obvious potty humor that goes along with the subject matter, the institution is a serious effort to pay tribute to the devices that made cities livable and prevented countless deaths from disease and plague. On display in the museum's two floors are toilets dating back to the nineteenth century, along with sinks, bathtubs, and tools of the toilet trade.

The museum also puts to rest many myths about sanitary plumbing. For example, you'll be relieved to know that Sir Thomas Crapper did not invent the toilet. (He did have a hand in making some of the innards of the tank.) As his name graced many a toilet, it became equated with its function.

When you've just gotta go, you'll find the museum at 39 Piedmont Street. You can take the toilet tour Tuesdays and Thursdays from 10:00 A.M. to 2:00 P.M. The museum is closed in July and August.

World Smile Day
Worcester

Commercial artist Harvey Ball believed that when you smile, the whole world smiles with you. He wanted to spread the message far and wide, and he succeeded beyond his wildest imagination. Today his Smiley design is one of the most recognized faces in the world and a universal symbol of good cheer.

On October 4. 2002, more than 750 people gathered on Worcester City
Hall Plaza to create the world's largest living smiley face, honoring
both Harvey Ball and World Smile Day IV.
Photo courtesy of Harvey Ball World Smile Corporation

In 1963 Ball, a native of Worcester, was asked by a local insurance company to design something to boost worker morale. The company had just merged with another firm and employees were unhappy with the move. Ball created Smiley, a face that was turned into pins and given to employees and clients. Since then the face has been featured on everything from underwear to yo-yos, stamps to T-shirts.

Although Harvey Ball was paid just $45 for his design, he was proud that his creation became the international symbol of good will. In 1999, when he felt his original message had become lost in the commercialization of Smiley, he created World Smile Day to restore the meaning of the symbol.

On the first Friday in October each year, World Smile Day is dedicated to good works and good cheer. The catch phrase for the day is, "Do an act of kindness. Help one person smile."

S U R E L Y   W E   J O U S T
Worcester

F air maidens in *amour* and their knights in shining armor
will feel right at home at the Higgins Armory Museum in
Worcester, Massachusetts. The museum is the only institution
in the Western Hemisphere dedicated solely to arms and armor,
and it is available for wedding receptions as well as birthday
party "OverKnights," when kids can suit up and really wreak
havoc. It's all in good joust, of course.

Those who really want to take in the knight life can take
lessons in medieval combat at the Higgins Armory Sword
Guild. We're told it is the only organization of its kind in the
world, and since they're armed and we're not, who are we to
argue with them?

Receptions are held in the Great Hall of the museum,
which is lined with scores of knights in armor and their steel-
plated steeds, some dating back to ancient Rome. The collection
of more than 4,000 artifacts includes swords, lances, maces,
and various other instruments of Asian and medieval mayhem.
There's even a hunting dog decked out in armor.

The Higgins collection also includes a real chastity belt, but
it is not considered appropriate to display and is locked away.

The Armory Museum began once upon a time (1929 to be
exact) when one of Worcester's leading industrialists, John
Woodman Higgins, a man of steel (he owned a steel mill) built a
four-story Gothic castle to house his personal collection of arms
and armor. The Art Deco building is one of the earliest in the

*Hunting dogs were sometimes outfitted with body armor to protect
them from antlers and tusks of stag and boar.*
Courtesy of the Higgins Armory Museum, Worcester, Massachusetts

nation to have an exterior constructed exclusively of steel and
glass. It is on the National Register of Historic Places.

The Higgins Armory Museum is located at 100 Barber
Avenue. For directions call (508) 853–6015 or log on to
www.higgins.org.

PITCHER PERFECT

*B*ack in 1880 baseball was a different game than the one we know today. Eight balls were a walk, the batter got to determine the strike zone, and the pitcher stood just 45 feet from the plate. And forget about eating sushi at the concession stands.

Still, whatever the differences, the record books show on June 12, 1880, that John Lee Richmond of the Worcester Ruby Legs (sometimes called the Brown Stockings) pitched the first perfect game in major league baseball. He beat the Cleveland Blues one to nothing, in what by all accounts was a nail-biter, delayed by rain in the ninth inning.

What makes Richmond's historic feat even more remarkable is that his perfect game in Worcester was actually the second game of two Richmond pitched that day . . . in two different states.

At the time Richmond was a senior at Brown University in Rhode Island and just four days from graduation. As was the tradition of the time, he had been up all night celebrating and had taken part in the traditional senior class

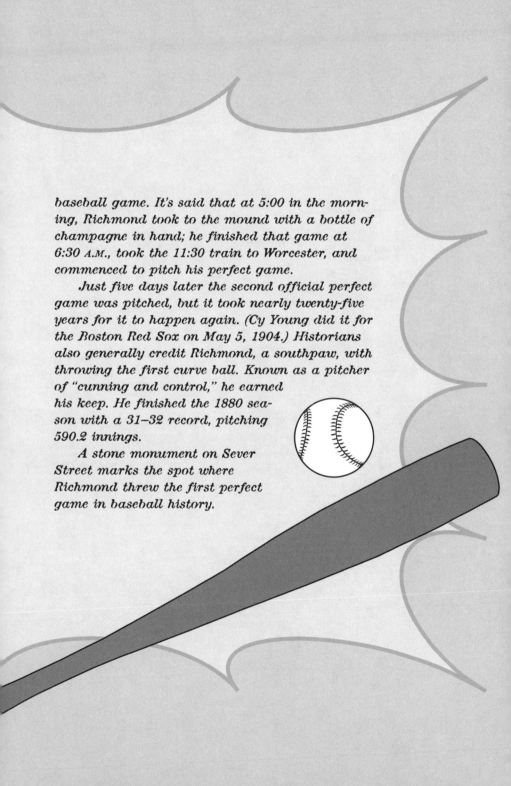

baseball game. It's said that at 5:00 in the morning, Richmond took to the mound with a bottle of champagne in hand; he finished that game at 6:30 A.M., took the 11:30 train to Worcester, and commenced to pitch his perfect game.

Just five days later the second official perfect game was pitched, but it took nearly twenty-five years for it to happen again. (Cy Young did it for the Boston Red Sox on May 5, 1904.) Historians also generally credit Richmond, a southpaw, with throwing the first curve ball. Known as a pitcher of "cunning and control," he earned his keep. He finished the 1880 season with a 31–32 record, pitching 590.2 innings.

A stone monument on Sever Street marks the spot where Richmond threw the first perfect game in baseball history.

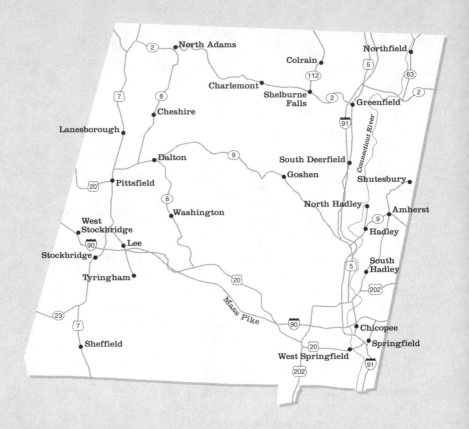

WEST MASSACHUSETTS, THE CONNECTICUT RIVER VALLEY, AND THE BERKSHIRES

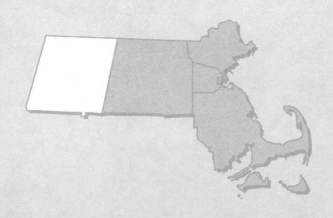

WEST MASSACHUSETTS, THE CONNECTICUT RIVER VALLEY, AND THE BERKSHIRES

BIG FEET
Amherst

Ever feel like you have two big left feet? Be glad that you weren't a dinosaur back in the Cretaceous period, when Tyrannosaurus Rex and other robust reptiles roamed. Imagine having one of those size-ninety-fives firmly planted on your toes while waltzing. But not all dinosaurs were that large. In the Jurassic age, no matter what the movies suggest, there's plenty of physical evidence that creatures were far smaller. To keep you in raptor attention, visit the Hitchcock Ichnology Collection in Amherst College's Pratt Museum. Ichnology, the study of fossilized footprints, is the focus of this especially fine group of more than 1,100 slabs. The collection, amassed by professor Edward Hitchcock, beginning in 1835, includes the world's most extensive series of dinosaur tracks, with examples ranging from 1 to 15 inches in length.

Why become the Imelda Marcos of the prehistoric set? Because footprints can reveal a wealth of information about the earth's early inhabitants, such as size, how quickly they moved, and even whether juveniles traveled by themselves. (The latter, presumably, would be proof of early malls.)

The museum is closed until sometime in 2006 because it's moving into a new building. But in the meantime, you can head over to the college's Frost Library, where the archives hold historical information about Hitchcock and the other academics associated with the collection. There's also an early catalog of the tracks and some photographs. Be sure to visit again when the facility reopens. After all, the fossils were millions of years in the making, so what is another year or two? For more information on the Pratt Museum, call (413) 542–2165 or visit www.amherst.edu/~pratt.

PICTURE PERFECT
Amherst

Some of us look at the latest bulging bestsellers and wish for simpler times, when men were men, women were women, and books were illustrated. Before moving on to Dostoyevsky, most people start their exposure to reading with picture books. These graphically evocative, deceptively simple tales pair a minimum of narration with engaging illustrations to help kids understand that, in the end, books are all about telling stories.

If you have a longing for less literature and more looking, then stop by the Eric Carle Museum of Picture Book Art. This is the first large museum—40,000 square feet, to be precise—devoted to kids' picture books. Carle's name may sound familiar if you've had young children in the last thirty years or so. He is a famous children's book illustrator, with such credits as *The Very Hungry Caterpillar* and *The Grouchy Ladybug*. (We wonder if, when in grade school, Carle submitted sheaves of drawings in lieu of book reports.) While there are Carle originals on display—what good is it if you can't exhibit at your own museum?—you can also take in the work of other noted American and international illustrators. The entrance fee is low, but don't plan to bring in food, drink, or pens and markers. (What, your parents never told you that you shouldn't scribble on the pictures?)

The museum is open year-round and even has free parking, a feature that is almost worth the trip in and of itself. For more information, call (413) 658–1100 or visit www.picturebookart .org. The museum is located at 125 West Bay Road.

O Y V E Y
A m h e r s t

I f you had to name a major center of Jewish culture outside the Middle East, what would you pick? If you said, "New York City," you would at least be in the right country. Given the subject of this book, you should certainly guess some place in Massachusetts. But the honor doesn't go to Boston or even Brockton or Sharon, all of which have a tradition of Jewish community. Instead, it goes to Amherst. What locked down the designation in 1997 was the opening of the 37,000-square-foot home for the National Yiddish Book Center.

The Center has become a big destination for Jewish tourists and claims to be visitor-friendly. No, the signs are not in Yiddish and English. Oy, our heads hurt from the thought. Maybe you don't know Yiddish (nor the Hebrew letters typically used for spelling), but it's worth some acquaintance. The sounds are

The National Yiddish Book Center hosts lectures, films, concerts, and live performances. Photo courtesy of Ned Gray

really intriguing. Yiddish is a language once shared by Jews all over Europe; it is derived from German, Hebrew, Aramaic, and several different Slavic and Romance languages. It is a language for schmoozing, a definite mish mash—a linguistic jumble. Yiddish is also probably the world's best language for cursing and lamenting the indignities of life.

The visitor center is free, open to the public, and offers gardens, exhibitions, and even an English-language bookstore. The Center also has research facilities.

To enjoy the National Yiddish Book Center, schlep over to Hampshire College at 893 West Street and ask for directions. To check whether you're trying to arrive on a Jewish holiday, or if you're *farblonzhet* (lost), call (413) 256–4900.

ALL IN THE FAMILY
Charlemont

How are you going to keep them down on the farm after they've seen Paris? That doesn't seem to be a problem at Avery's general store, where five generations of the same family have been occupied since the business opened in 1861, with the sixth already hanging around. Do those Avery family members who stay at the store get chained in place?

The term *general store* does not do justice to this establishment—it's packed with almost every conceivable type of item, from custom-cut meats and organic maple syrup to hardware, paints, and clothing. The store, more officially called A. L. Avery and Son, brings everything to the town that the residents might want. A good thing, too, as few towns with a population under 1,500 can attract a mall. But Avery's offers a service you won't find at a mall: Every Friday there is a delivery run for homebound customers. You will find A. L. Avery and Son on 16 Main Street. Just don't bring pictures of Paris—you wouldn't want to tempt tradition.

THE CHEESE WHIZZES
Cheshire

Cheshire was established by the first non-Puritans in the area—the founders were descended from followers of Roger Williams, who had headed off to Rhode Island in the mid-1600s in search of religious freedom. Perhaps they inherited his rebellious streak, for when a young United States of America voted for its third president, in 1800, Cheshire was the only town in that part of the state that sided with Thomas Jefferson—unanimously. Driven on by Elder John Ireland, the local preacher, the dissidents for once managed to align themselves with the winning party, and they wanted to celebrate. Fun back then wasn't quite the same as our current concept. The dissidents lived in dairy country, and someone had the bright idea of creating a giant wheel of cheese—Cheshire, to be precise. The town worked hard, gathering curds from every resident farmer and pressing them into a wheel totaling 4 feet across, 1½ feet thick, and 1,235 pounds in weight. It took six horses pulling a sled to bring the slab to a ship on the Hudson River, which then brought it to Washington, D.C. (Maybe the town fathers hoped to have their whey with the president.)

It took a few months for the appetizer to reach Jefferson. The president was duly impressed and put it on display in the East Room of the White House in January 1802, with Supreme Court justices, foreign diplomats, and Congress looking on. Federalist critics of Jefferson tried to make fun of the cheese as a trivial interest and not worthy of the country's attention. In doing so, they compared the big cheese to the recent unearthing of mastodon bones in New York. (The excavation, which had taken place with aid from the Jefferson administration, was another unworthy endeavor in the eyes of the critics.) These writers called the wheel the *mammoth cheese,* giving rise to a new adjective. (Never underestimate the power of cheese.) Jefferson, unfazed, responded to the town with a personal letter.

In the twentieth century, town residents decided to commemorate their earlier commemoration. In 1940 they created a monument, a concrete cheese press, in memory of "the big Cheshire cheese." You can see it for yourself near the intersection of School and Church Streets.

RULING THE ROOST
Cheshire

In his time, FDR promised Americans a chicken in every pot. Today the people of Cheshire would be hard-pressed to find a pot that was big enough. Apparently the people in this town, who also have that memorial to a giant cheese, have an affinity for big food. Sitting atop the town's Country Charm restaurant is a statue of a rooster standing about 10 feet tall, according to staff. Over the years many small businesses have had the idea that creating some sort of unusual decoration would help attract business. What hatched this particular bird was the Chicken Stop, a restaurant that previously occupied the premises.

The rooster stood proudly on the grass in front of the Chicken Stop and then the Country Charm until college students abducted the mascot in the mid-1990s. Perhaps the whole lot of them were trying to fly the coop. But sanity—and the rooster—returned, the latter being relegated to the roof where a casual acquaintance could not easily turn into a pickup. To see the proud poultry, visit the Country Charm on Route 8. But if you're hungry, don't go before 11:00 A.M., as it doesn't serve breakfast. Apparently this particular rooster doesn't rise at the crack of dawn.

CHAMPIONSHIP CHILLING
Chicopee

K now that saying, "Save room for dessert"? Here's one treat
that would have required, oh, about fifty-odd years of judi-
cious eating. Many people have done some extreme and down-
right crazy things for an entry into the *Guinness Book of
Records*. Owners of the Dairy Queen in Chicopee decided that it
would only be natural to try for the title of largest blended
dessert on July 1, 1999. This frozen feat was a mass of vanilla
ice cream (or whatever it is that Dairy Queens serve) with a
copious amount of crushed Oreo cookies. The sweet treat
topped out at a walloping 5,316.6 pounds. And you thought
that a brownie sundae at the local family restaurant was a
challenge. Undoubtedly Jenny Craig is still having psychically
induced nightmares from it.

Actually, "largest blended dessert" sounds a bit dull. We
think that *Guinness* missed the banana-split boat by ignoring a
more apt title: biggest brain freeze. The post-entrée entry was
too large to host at the shop, so it made its debut at the nearby
Riverside Amusement Park in Agawam, now part of the local
Six Flags theme park. You can still see the shop that created
the confection at 1535 Memorial Drive, or call (413) 535–3005.
Don't be surprised, however, if service is slow; we are sure that
some of the staff is still recovering.

BRIDGE OVER TROUBLED WATERS
Colrain

Few bridges jump around the way the Arthur B. Smith covered bridge has. The peripatetic pathway started its history in the 1800s in one location. Then a reconfiguration of some roads made it unnecessary. Transportation's discard was the boon of farmer Arthur Smith, who had been driving his cows across an open bridge to pasture lands. But that structure had collapsed, giving his cattle what was probably their first and only bath.

The existing covered bridge was moved to aid Smith and served him well. Years later, when Smith was no longer in the agriculture business, a major local employer—a cider mill—needed a bridge to move its product across the river. Again the covered bridge was moved, taking Smith's name with it. (Are you feeling dislocated yet?)

The bridge enjoyed a relatively long period of stability until 1981, although it did suffer some deterioration. No surprise, as any of us would have worn down a bit after 150 years. Now on the National Register of Historic Places, the bridge could not simply be disassembled and turned into firewood. The Colrain Historical Society involved itself and the town worked hard, supporting an effort to raise $40,000 to repair and move the bridge yet again, this time to a corn field. A local logger donated his efforts and the state offered lumber from a nearby forest.

It was an example of civic efficiency—until the wood had been obtained. Then one delay after another occurred. Some residents claim that someone misappropriated a portion of the raised funds. The Historical Society opposed suggestions to make the structure a footbridge and insisted that the bridge be used for vehicle travel only. During all the arguing, the replacement wood, sitting under a tarp next to the bridge, eventually rotted.

Today there are still plans to renovate the bridge. But now that the Massachusetts Highway Department is involved, the project is estimated to run $1.2 billion. And there is still no way to cross the river at the spot that was to benefit from the restoration and relocation. Was it highway robbery? Or just the case of a bridge not far enough? You can usually see the bridge from Route 112, but if the corn is high, go to the end of Lydonville Road.

L O N G   M A Y   I T   G L O W
C o l r a i n

N eon artist Tony Palumbo moved to Colrain with his partner, Michael Collins, in 1994. As electrically charged art is not a major industry in this part of Massachusetts, the two opened a well-received upscale restaurant, the Green Emporium. But you know what they say about neon—it's in the blood, or tubes. No matter; Palumbo couldn't keep away from bending the light. So he kept producing art, with a number of galleries exhibiting his work. Fast forward to September 19, 2001, right after the attacks on the World Trade Center. Local farmer Kenny Shearer stopped to talk with Palumbo and the conversation turned to the recent tragic event. Palumbo, a native New Yorker, was feeling badly and Shearer said that he had thought of erecting a large flag on his own property. Suddenly the switch flipped on for Palumbo, who asked, "Why not neon?"

The two got to work, getting permission from town selectmen and obtaining a building permit. Shearer drew to scale what he had envisioned. Turns out that when he thinks, he thinks *big*. The flag he had envisioned was to be 28 feet wide and 16 feet high. More people got involved. Shearer enlisted his friends and family, and an electrician neighbor donated his time to do all the electrical wiring. Palumbo's assistant, Scott Hoffman, joined in. Neon tubing came from Palumbo's studio in Brooklyn, and he trucked the 350 feet of powdered tubing himself. The local electrical utility, WMECO, helped by donating the power cable, while E. W. Martin Electric dug the trench. Obviously the Colrain crew was charged up over the project. You might think that art, when political, is usually hypercritical, but this is one time when it was deeply moved by current events.

Palumbo's installation, *Glowing Glory*, was officially lighted on November 25, 2001. You can see the flag online at www.glowingglory.com. For the real thing, use Palumbo's directions: From exit 26 off Interstate 91, take Route 2 west for 3.5 miles, turn right (north) onto Colrain/Shelburne Road, drive 2 miles to the Colrain/Shelburne line, then look left at Coombs Hill Road. Keep your head up and you can't miss it. Want to take a bit of the flag with you? Chandler's General Store in Colrain, 7 Jacksonville Road, carries postcards. You don't even need a plug.

R A G S   T O   R I C H E S
D a l t o n

T here are people who dream of wading through piles of money. We can relate, but short of either being employed by the U.S. Mint or being adopted by the likes of Bill Gates, the closest you might get is the Crane Museum of Papermaking. While you won't see the finished product, you can learn a great deal about the paper that our money is printed on. Crane sold paper to Paul Revere in 1775, who printed the first paper money in what was then the Colonies, and it has regularly provided stock for American currency since 1842. In 1844 Crane developed a technique for weaving silk threads in banknotes to

The Crane Museum of Papermaking traces the history
of Amerian papermaking from rags to riches.
Photo courtesy of Crane & Co. Inc.

help deter counterfeiters; more recently it has patented the
technique of putting in those identifying security threads.
Even though the company knows where the money is, Crane
also produces stationery and paper for digital printing.

Instead of using wood pulp like most mills, Crane continues
to produce papers with high rag content for strength and
beauty. And you thought cotton was just for blue jeans. You
can learn about how the company has historically made paper
and see old paper molds and other educational displays at the
museum in Crane's Old Stone Mill, built in 1844 on 30 South
Street (413–684–6481). Oh, and as for that banknote paper—
sorry, but no samples.

KILLER BEAVERS

Beavers are known as the engineers of the animal world, not as predatory killers. At least,
that's their reputation until you get out to parts
of western Massachusetts, where Indian legends
tell a different story. According to the Pocumtuck
tribe of Deerfield, a giant beaver lived in a lake,
now long gone, that was once in the area. Apparently the buck-toothed wonder, tired of wearing
down its incisors chewing wood, would from time
to time venture into the surrounding area and
eat people.

This was not a habit to endear the creature
to the Pocumtuck. According to their legends, the
people requested the aid of another giant—the
spirit Hobomock, who hunted the beaver and
killed it. The beaver sank back into the lake,
transforming from animal into rock. After the
lake drained, over time, the carcass was left
exposed. There are legends from some other
nearby tribes that mirror the basic story, varying
some details, such as what Hobomock used to
smite the amphibious rodent.

These days, the beaver's body is
what we call the Pocumtuck Range
and the head is Mount Sugarloaf,
now a popular ski resort.

TUNNEL TO NOWHERE
Goshen

U nexplained natural structures may be mysterious, but they are at least understandable in some remote, prehistoric way. It's when something unnatural is more recent, when you would think that there must be some record of the effort involved, that the unknown can be plain annoying. In those terms the Goshen Tunnel is extremely irritating and confusing.

In the nineteenth century, some hunters came upon a big hole in the ground, more than 3 feet in diameter. The opening runs straight down about 15 feet. At the bottom, two tunnels, about 2-feet tall, run parallel to the surface in two different directions. One of them is another 15 feet or so in length, while the other extends five times as far. Both end at cave-ins. It's a tidy hole, lined with rock and flagstones, so obviously someone spent considerable time and energy creating it.

But why? On that point, there is only conjecture. Recently people have started calling it the counterfeiter's den, because authorities once apprehended some practitioners of that art a few miles away. However, it is hard to imagine a counterfeiter creating such an elaborate hideaway with no light and little room to run a printing press. Others hypothesize that some settler in the area was trying to raise silkworms, or that some- one in the Underground Railroad took the term too seriously. However, some research indicates that parts of the tunnels were dug about 10,000 years ago and that the stone ceiling was put into place around 3,000 B.C. Given the age, we think that the tunnels were actually an early relic of the Big Dig, the project that is (at this writing) still depressing the central artery of Boston underground—and depressing everyone who must put up with it. Any century now, the link between there and Goshen is bound to open up. In the meantime, to view the site (the entrance is usually blocked for safety), take a trip to the Goshen Cemetery off Williams Drive between Cape Street and Route 9.

GREEN POWER
Greenfield

I f you are convinced that one more visit to an enclosed educational enclave with meaningful content (a.k.a., a museum) will require medical professionals to drag you away kicking and screaming, it's time to run away and out into the open air at the Greenfield Energy Park. Whoever designed this place must have remembered what it was like to be a kid.

Kids blow off steam on a wooden play train.
Photo by Sandy Thomas/Courtesy of Greenfield Energy Park

Yes, it seems a bit politically correct to expect youngsters to frolic amid large solar panels and dance between the batteries. But don't be harsh. You'll soon be entranced by a sculpture of a train powered by an on-site electrical grid with figures that pop up and down on the hour. There's another sculpture that turns by wind energy, and custom tiles that identify trees and shrubs around the park. The amphitheater is made of recycled granite, and the transportation museum is housed in an old train caboose.

Perhaps the best attractions are the wooden play train and the butterfly garden, where your kids can blow off steam. To arrive for your day of fascination, take your favorite environmentally friendly transportation to the park on Bank Row, also on the Web at www.nesea.org/park.

GRAVE RUBBERS
Greenfield

Does history leave you cold? Not as cold as the subjects of this organization's focus. The Association for Gravestone Studies thinks that much of history is written in stone—headstones, to be specific. They see important information—from genealogy and religious history to changing fashions in art and literature—locked into the letters at the tops of burial sites.

Any of the association's 1,200 members can check with the central registry to get information on gravestone subjects. The association has a lending library of reference volumes and an online store with instructions on how to do research on the occupant of a particular grave. The association also offers cemetery guides, calendars, note cards with images of gravestones in the snow (be careful whom you send these to), and

This organization hopes to rub you the right way.
Photo by Robert Posson/Courtesy of the Association for
Gravestone Studies

even software for recording details of gravestones. Information
kits give you the practical instructions on how to do everything from making gravestone rubbings to understanding
symbols on the stones to learning techniques for analyzing
cemetery data.

For more information, call (413) 772–0836 or go to
www.gravestonestudies.org. The organization's headquarters
are at 278 Main Street, Suite 207.

WHAT COMES DOWN MUST GO UP
Greenfield

I sn't it nice to know that some things don't change? For example, the trusty law of gravity is bound to bring things to their lowest point. Well, it will, *most* of the time. If you're the type who likes to know about exceptions to the rule, head over to Greenfield and take the exit off Route 91 for Gravity Hill. According to legend, a horrible accident happened there, involving a bus full of children going off the overpass, killing all the occupants. As the story goes, if you stop a car beneath the overpass and take it out of gear, the phantom children's hands will push the vehicle down the road a bit so that you won't get hurt.

Okay, so the story might seem a bit hard to believe. But many people who've tried it have found that their cars rolled at least a good 20 feet in a direction that seemed to be uphill. If you are interested in trying to bend gravity to somebody else's will, or just experiencing a good optical illusion, take Route 91 to exit 26. Turn so you can drive under the overpass, shift into neutral, and wait to see what happens.

ON BALANCE
Lanesborough

K eeping on your toes will be easy after a visit to Balance Rock. This massive piece of limestone, 25 feet by 15 feet by 10 feet weighing some 165 tons, perches delicately on another

SUPERNATURAL CITIZENS

*F*or some reason, Hadley seems to have attracted the worst and the best of the supernatural. We have all heard someone describe a woman as a "witch" when what they are really thinking involves a simple substitute of the initial letter. We wonder whether that might be what provoked the denunciation of Mary Webster, the Witch of Hadley. She reputedly had an unpleasant temper under the best of conditions. After a life of poverty and social shunning, she had a tongue ready to attack those who drew her displeasure.

Some of Webster's neighbors decided that she must be a witch. They blamed her for scaring cattle and children, among other things. At a time when accusations were almost as good as proof, she was brought before a local court, sent on to Boston, and held over for further trial. Yet ultimately she was found not guilty by a jury. (Perhaps they thought they would be safer were she back from whence she came.)

Back in Hadley, Webster's neighbors disagreed with the judgment. A group of young men dragged her from her house, attempted to hang her, then tossed her in the snow. Being a tough old bird, she lived another eleven years and died of old age at around seventy. If they thought she was a witch before, we'd hate to see what she was like after.

Hadley also had an angel—William Goffe. He was one of the fifty-nine judges who signed the death warrant of Charles I of England, endearing none of them to Charles II. Both Goffe and fellow judge Edward Whaley had to flee to the New World in 1660 and go into hiding.

After a few years of moving about, the two were hidden by the Rev. John Russell for sixteen years. It is said that once, when a group of Indians were attacking the Colonists, an aged man, unknown to any of the group of fifty or so families, took charge. He repelled the braves and then vanished. The people said that it was an angel sent to protect them, but the legend claims that it was Goffe, who had left his hiding place to lend aid and then disappeared as soon as the fight was over. Unfortunately, later scholarship disputes that Indian forces ever approached the town and suggests that the "angel of Hadley" story started in the eighteenth century. We consider it a case of miraculous conscription.

rock 3 feet above the ground. You'd think it was a shaky position, and it is—touch the rock and it shivers—but it hasn't come down yet.

This wasn't some invention by a tipsy architect, but rather a natural result of glacial action. That might explain why stories about the boulder go back centuries. In the 1800s it was owned by the Hubert family, who welcomed those who came to gawk. Then a traveling band of rascals who asked to see the rock promptly set up shop and tried to charge others a dime each for the view. Grove Hubert, the family member in charge at the time, was angry enough to try to rock the rock. Luckily, he learned that oxen do little when it comes to moving large chunks of mineral.

Eventually the state purchased the property and planted tens of thousands of trees to make it an inviting park. There are some other interesting rocks here, too: a rock that looks like a whale, one with a series of cracks that look like a cross, and a pair of twin rocks.

On balance, we know it's only a rock that doesn't roll, but we like it. See the stone at Balance Rock State Park on Balance Rock Road in the northwest corner of Pittsfield State Forest. For more information, visit www.state.ma.us/dem/parks/pitt .htm.

FACE FACTS
Lanesborough

Ever had that funny feeling that someone is watching you? That is what happened to residents in northwest Massachusetts from May 10 through May 14, 1990. Heavy rains throughout that time finally sent earth, granite, and everything else tumbling down the side of nearby Mount Greylock, revealing the image of a face on the slope of this tallest peak in the state. In sort of a reverse face lift, the rough visage of an Indian appeared, staring down. People started calling the figure Chief Greylock, after a Waronoke Indian who spent a good part of his time in the early 1700s harassing English soldiers from a secret cave in the mountain. At one point, he had half his foot amputated after a run-in with an animal trap; little wonder that he gained the nickname "the frowning chief of the Waronokes." But apparently that didn't slow him down. He sided with the French during the French and Indian Wars and was never caught or defeated, although he did manage to humiliate English forces time and again.

You can find the Mount Greylock State Reservation on Rockwell Road in Lanesborough. Bascom Lodge, at the top, offers a place to stay overnight as well as food in the summer and fall. Call (413) 499–4262 for more information.

THIS IS THE CHURCH, THIS IS THE STEEPLE

Lee

Record-tall buildings are usually the province of corporations. But for some reason, the First Congregational Church in Lee has come out on top in the area of timber frame construction— that's where the skeleton of the building is a series of large posts and beams that interlock. It's a beautiful style of building to see because the frame is exposed on the interior, adding not only great strength but also aesthetic pleasure.

For the First Congregation Church building, the timber construction is in the 105-foot-tall spire. It is the highest structure in the country using this method of construction. But remember, we're talking about the steeple—the very top of the church, a needle point rising even above the church bells, which are above the four-faced clock (itself a curiosity because it is wound by hand and runs for seven days before needing another winding). Sitting atop the rest of the church, the steeple reaches 192 feet high. In other words, this is a part of the church that rarely receives visitors.

However, some people have had a look. Built in 1857, the steeple had been struck by lightning and by 1987 needed some repair. (What kind of makeover do you think *you* might need at the age of 150?) Besides other bits of maintenance, it seems that the tower was tilting a couple of feet. Over a period of two weeks, Dalton-based Hill-Engineers, Architects, Planners, Inc. used hydraulic jacks to move some columns up an eighth of an inch a day. Presumably, they wanted to avoid moving too quickly and causing a need to yell "timberrrrrrrr." To see the no-longer-tipping tower, head to 25 Park Place.

ACTION MAN
North Adams

N orman Rockwell was known for his highly realistic style of illustrations of everyday life. No surprise that his son Jarvis was also drawn to the visual. But the younger Rockwell had a more playful attitude and the toys to prove it. Since 1979, Rockwell has been collecting toys—specifically, action figures ranging from an inch to a foot in height. We're talking enough toys to fill eight large containers in storage at a moving company, sixty or seventy used liquor boxes at a storage facility, and even more in the attic of his home. No one has counted how many there are, though Rockwell has started a list. So far, his list, complete with descriptions and locations, fills six looseleaf notebooks. "I think they're extraordinary," he

Jarvis Rockwell's action figures fill an 11-foot-high, four-sided pyramid.

Photo by Robert B. Wyatt/Courtesy of Jarvis Rockwell

says of his toys. "They represent where we are, what we think as we go along. They're endlessly inventive. Even watching the way they change the Hulk figure—how big can you make him? I just keep buying them."

At one time in the past, Rockwell invited passersby off the street to come into his home and pick a toy to take with them. But that was unsatisfying, so he created a piece of conceptual art using thousands of the figures arranged around an 11-foot-high, four-sided pyramid. The sculpture is now in storage at the Massachusetts Museum of Contemporary Art. When the museum's sixth building is opened sometime in the next couple of years, the pyramid—called Maya, after the Hindu concept of the illusion of the world—will again be on exhibit.

Rockwell isn't getting any younger—he's in his early seventies at the time of this writing—and he'd like to do something with many of the figures in storage. So don't be surprised if you hear about him toying with more art.

THE BIG SHOW
North Adams

W here would you go for contemporary art? New York? L.A.? Chicago? San Francisco? How about an old textile town in northwest Massachusetts with a population hovering around 15,000? North Adams is home to the Massachusetts Museum of Contemporary Art, or Mass MoCA—the largest American museum devoted to the genre.

How such an institution found itself in an economically depressed region of the commonwealth is an interesting story that starts in 1988, when then-governor Michael Dukakis earmarked funds for the project. The idea was to provide an economic transfusion to the region. Then "the Duke" had his picture taken while wearing a helmet and sitting in a tank, and not long after, he lost his presidential bid. The Massachusetts economic "miracle" turned out to be a temporary turn of events, money became tight, and gubernatorial successor William Weld froze the funds. But in 1995 he finally approved a large sum of money to begin converting old textile mills into galleries and theaters. These days, Mass MoCA sprawls among twenty-six nineteenth-century factory buildings on a thirteen-acre campus and covers not only the visual arts, but electronic media and the performing arts as well. Included amid the 100,000 square feet of exhibition space is a single gallery that is as long as a football field; undoubtedly, some artist will bring in two eleven-man teams and make the project interactive by selling beer and hot dogs.

Natalie Jeremijenko's Tree Logic *greets visitors to Mass MoCA.*
Photo by Doug Bartow/Courtesy of Mass MoCA

It seems equivalent to finding a major league baseball sta-
dium in the middle of a wheat field. But Mass MoCA seems to
be thriving on the concept that "if you build it, they will come."
With theaters, outdoor cinemas, workshops, and even companies subletting office and retail space, this is almost a mall-as-
art project. You can see plays, hear music, dine at restaurants,
and even bring the kids to a family gallery and studio space
called Kidspace at Mass MoCA. You can probably even get lost
and organize your own rescue expedition. Check the days and
hours for Kidspace at www.massmoca.org/kidspace or at (413)
662-2111. You can get information on the parent organization
by calling the same phone number or by visiting www.mass
moca.org. To tour the main galleries, head to 87 Marshall
Street; Kidspace is at 1032 Mass MoCA Way. Bring your own
football helmet.

LOST ITS MARBLE
North Adams

I f you can take slang literally, then North Adams must be one of the craziest places in Massachusetts, having lost a lot of its marble. No, not *marbles*—we're talking about white marble, the stuff used in hearthstones and fireplace mantels and cemeteries. For more than a century, the area now called Natural Bridge State Park was the leading source for the material used throughout Massachusetts.

The famous author Nathaniel Hawthorne wrote in 1838 that parts of North Adams seemed gloomy and stern to him. Well, of course, Nat; we're talking the essence of fancy headstones here. The marble owes its quality in part to its chemical makeup: 98 percent calcium carbonate, otherwise known as limestone or natural chalk (or the antacid pills you might pop into your mouth after a bad burrito). Not only is the material beautiful and suited for building, but the dust and chips left after slicing slabs were also put into toothpaste, putty, and soap. How versatile: You can get your hands dirty cutting it, then wash with it afterward.

From 1837 to 1947 the mill literally ground out all these products, eventually shipping 400,000 pounds of stone a day. Then came a fire, putting the mill out of business and leaving the place as quiet as a mausoleum. A man by the name of Edward Elder purchased the upscale rock pit from the company that had owned it, and he ran it as a tourist attraction until his death in the mid-1980s. Shortly afterwards, his widow sold the site to the Massachusetts Department of Environmental Management, which turned it into a park.

One of the interesting features is a natural marble bridge. (Hence the name.) For more information, see www.berkshire web.com/mohawktrail/natbridge.html, or call either (413)

663–6392 (May to October) or (413) 663–6312 (November to
April.) To cross to Natural Bridge State Park, drive north on
Route 8 half a mile from downtown North Adams.

GETTING KIDDED
Northfield

Ahoy, matey. *Ahhhrrrr,* you'd think that a pirate's story
would take place on the ocean. Last map we checked, this
part of Massachusetts is some 90 miles from the Atlantic. So
why would anyone associate raiders of the high seas with
Northfield? The legend goes that Captain Kidd actually sailed
here up the Connecticut River, trying to find a hiding place for
his loot. After all, even in the early eighteenth century, it was
difficult to walk into a bank with chests of stolen goods to
make a deposit.

So Kidd and some compatriots supposedly buried a chest of
gold somewhere on Northfield's Clark's Island. That alone
might sound suspicious, as the Connecticut River is often too
shallow in spots for any boat, let along one carrying a chest of
gold coins.

According to the stories from Temple and Sheldon's *History
of Northfield, MA, 150 Years,* Kidd and a few of his crew managed to make their way to Clark's Island at a part called Pine
Meadow. They supposedly buried a treasure chest and left.
After the hangman's noose snagged Kidd, the treasure was left
to be found. A legend grew that the only way to find the gold
was to have three people dig soundlessly under a full moon
that was directly overhead. In the 1800s a trio of men reportedly was digging about under these conditions, not even swat-
ting the mosquitoes that were munching them (for fear of
making noise), when they spotted a chest. Someone spoke in

elation, at which point the money sank out of reach, never to be found again.

Feel the need to dig into the legend more? Maybe you will be the one who finds the treasure. At some point cartographers took the legend seriously enough to rechristen Clark's Island as Kidd's Island. It's roughly in the middle of the river along-side a spot about half a mile down from the northern start of Pine Meadow Road. Bring your own boat—and be very quiet. You're hunting treasure.

D E R B Y   D A Y
Pittsfield

T raditional 4-H fairs are a staple of rural areas, including much of western Massachusetts. Youths compete by exhibit-ing vegetables, flowers, and even livestock they have raised. But while the Berkshire County *4-H Fair Handbook for 2004* states how much cleanliness—both of animals and the areas in which they are kept—contributes to scores awarded by judges, there is a delicate lack of mention of the annual dung drop derby.

The derby is an annual fundraiser. Fair organizers and workers divide a field into a large grid. People purchase a square for $5.00, much as they might buy a raffle ticket. A cow is turned loose in the field, where it is welcome to stroll around, chew its cud . . . and drop a cow patty. The person who wagered on that square is the winner. It's not clear what hap-pens if the deposit drops on the border between two grids.

Unfortunately, there have been times when the cow simply wouldn't cooperate, at which point another is brought in. It might seem udderly silly to you, but we have it on good authority that locals anticipate the event. To find the next derby, check the Massachusetts listings of agricultural fairs at www.state.ma.us/dfa/fairs/fair_list.htm. Go to the youth fairs section, then look for the Berkshire County 4-H Fair. You can also call (413) 448–8285 for more information. The fair itself runs one day, usually the third Saturday in August, and can be found at Utility Drive, which is off Holmes Road. Needless to say, don't wear your good clothes.

SING, SING, SING
Sheffield

D o inveterate shower singers make you wish that the ring around the tub was a wringing of a neck? If you want to K-O people who start bellowing, "O-K-L-A-H-O-M-A . . . Oklahoma!" then by all means, be wary of Sheffield in the summer, when it hosts the Berkshire Choral Festival. Started in 1982 and running on the campus of the Berkshire School, the festival attracts 1,600 people from all over the world who have an insatiable desire to burst into song and want to spend a week doing nothing but that. They call it "the week that lasts a lifetime," and we have a funny feeling that we would agree with them. Participants come from an even larger pool, and would-be choristers must enter a drawing by February to get a spot on the roster. Warning: This event is not over in seven days. Professional conductors switch off to provide a season that lasts for about five weeks.

If you'd like to sing classical works in intensive rehearsal periods under accomplished conductors, this place might be for you. Just make sure you are vocally in shape. The choral music is moderately difficult, and if you don't know how to keep to your part—whether soprano, alto, tenor, baritone, or bass—the music lovers around you may cease to be lovable. You have to

study tapes and written music ahead of time, and if management thinks that your singing is not up to snuff, they reserve
the right to kick you out on your andante. If you like singing
but have a voice that depresses even the tone deaf, you can still
attend . . . as a member of the audience. For more information,
call (413) 229–8526 or visit www.chorus.org.

*B*RIDGE OVER *T*ROUBLED *L*ILACS
Shelburne Falls

T here are people who will turn *anything* into a planter, but
most are amateurs compared to the folks in Shelburne
Falls. These gardening gurus took an old trolley bridge and
transformed it into a garden. And this isn't some little stone
structure adorned by a few gladioluses and petunias. The
Bridge of Flowers runs some 400 feet, with 500 varieties of
flowers that start blooming in April and end in October in a
floral last hurrah of chrysanthemums. Originally built in
1908, this piece of civil engineering was as staid as any water-
works or highway overpass. It was the property of the Shelburne Falls and Colrain Street Railway and part of the route of
the freight trolley that operated between this town and the
mills in nearby Colrain.

But progress reared its ugly head as the automobile made
way for its big brother, the truck. Suddenly it was cheaper and
easier to make runs between the towns with individual vehicles
and not maintain an entire train system; the rail company
went out of business in 1928. Sure, there was no problem taking the cars off the tracks, pretending that the entire venture
never existed, but a bridge is a hard thing to hide, especially
when water mains run across it. To keep from being high and
dry, the town bought the bridge in 1929. Some locals thought

that there was no reason that something so utilitarian had to
look seedy. If water was going to run over the bridge, they rea-
soned, they might as well sprinkle some *on* it. That year, the
town raised money to transform the bridge into a public garden. (Undoubtedly, this was before the great stock market
crash, which left few people with a pot to plant in.) Since then,
donations and a largely volunteer effort have kept the bridge in
bloom and the weeds at bay. Today the Shelburne Falls Women's
Club does much of the work, along with a hired gardener. For
more information, call (413) 625-2544 or just travel to the
intersection of Water and Bridge Streets—how appropriate—to
see the floral frenzy.

P R E H I S T O R I C   P O T H O L E S
S h e l b u r n e   F a l l s

I f you've ever made pothole jokes like, "Oh, this one is so big
that it almost swallowed my car," take time to visit Shelburne
Falls and see what real potholes are like. These aren't the measly
little pits that dot pavements after a cold snap. The biggest of
them ranks as the world's largest pothole, 39 feet across. Not
only could you literally lose your car in this mother of all pot-
holes, you could probably say goodbye to a good-sized truck.

Luckily for the residents, the potholes are not on the streets
but down near a hydroelectric dam. It seems that during the
time of the last glaciers melting, the region's level of high
water was quite impressive and the Connecticut River greatly
expanded its reach. Stones, trapped in a riverbed, were shaken
about by the flow of water and acted as drills. They created the
potholes near the dam.

You might think it strange for a town to look at a collection
of old holes in the ground and consider it a tourist attraction.

Even stranger is that people actually *do* come by to see the pot-holes. Residents have even given them a name: the Glacial Pot-holes. (Better that than the Pits.) Go to the end of Deerfield Street and you will find an observation deck overlooking the potholes, as well as some local falls. Just get there before some zealous department of public works makes a pilgrimage and leaves a mass of asphalt.

S IMPLE OR S IMPLE - M INDED ?
Shutesbury

Eugenics is the dubious pursuit of using genetics to argue for the supposed superiority of groups of people. Although it turned into a horror in World War II, before that it actually had proponents in the United States. And the evidence they waved about was actually garnered from Shutesbury, a sleepy town of under 2,000 that hasn't any stores. As explained in an interesting story in *Boston Magazine* (www.bostonmagazine .com/special1/eugenics_1202.shtml), the Shutesbury Study of 1928 was a deceptive inquiry into the personal, medical, and educational histories of the residents. It was used as evidence for the necessity of culling society's undesirables. Getting shameful support from leading academics from such schools as Harvard as well as others less "qualified" (the man who arranged the study, Leon Whitney, was actually a dog breeder), the movement gained attention for its views at the time. Much of the evidence came from field studies where peo-ple were supposedly trained to detect human character by appearance. One of the proponents, Walter Fernald, was the first resident superintendent of the Massachusetts School for the Feeble-Minded, an institution that would eventually take his name and go on to greater fame by feeding radioactive cereal to children in the 1950s as part of another experiment. Yet Shutesbury seems to have survived it all. People still live there, the air is clean, the traffic is insignificant, and the surroundings are beautiful. When you come from a congested urban locale, it makes you wonder who the simple-minded people are after all.

F E E , F I E , F O E , F O O T
S o u t h   H a d l e y

M any youngsters are interested in dinosaurs, and for a few, the fascination never ends. In the case of the Nash family, you might say that dinosaurs became an obsession that turned into a vocation. The business used to be called Nash Dino Land, but when the founder, Carlton Nash, died a few years ago, his son, Kornell, changed the name to the Nash Dinosaur Track Quarry.

Dinosaur tracks go back a long time in the area. (Okay, okay, they go back a long time *everywhere*.) But it was in 1802 that people found the first prehistoric footprints in the South Hadley area. For some reason, during the Jurassic period the roaming lizards were ill-bred, walking through the local mud flats and never wiping their feet. Such is the way of the world that one man's messy ground can be another man's living. Growing up in the area, Carlton Nash was fascinated with dinosaurs. Right after high school he began prowling through the local woods, hoping to unearth a cache of footprints. He found one in 1933, but it took him six years to save enough money to buy the property.

The elder Nash began working his track mine. It must have felt as though he was on a treadmill: At first he cut Christmas trees in the fall, worked for the electric company in the spring,

and sold dinosaur prints in the summer. By 1950 he was able
to make dinosaurs his business. His son eventually joined him,
and now Kornell spends his time trying to update displays that
are showing their ages. (Though after the first million years,
who notices a decade or two?) Much of Kornell's living comes
from selling two groups of actual fossil prints: one about 4 to 7
inches, and the other about 12 to 20 inches. Prices start at $50
and go to roughly $1,000, depending on the size of the track
and the condition. It must be said that he prices by the foot.

Nash Dinosaur Track Quarry is just off Route 116, about 3
miles north of South Hadley Center. Look for the sign.

SEUSS I AM
Springfield

That Dr. Seuss, that Dr. Seuss, you cannot fault that Dr.
Seuss. Could he, would he illustrate? Books for kids would
seem his fate. And his words were always pat. He could write
about a cat. He could top the cat with a hat from the desk at
which he sat. Kids would laugh and that was that.

Before he found his kids' book fame, young Ted Geisel's job
was tame, marketing a corporate name. After this came work
more rare, magazines requiring care: *Judge* and *Life* and *Van-
ity Fair.* Then he got to draw and write; publishers had seen
his light, work that was a pure delight. Raves from critics it
did woo: Emmys, Oscars, Pulitzer, too.

When he died, his hometown thought, "Celebrate," and so
they sought something fun, not overwrought. Artist Lark Grey
Dimond-Cates was called in, to craft bronze statues thick and
thin. These show Dr. Seuss, cat in tow, Yertle Turtle, Grinch, and
Max, Horton's Who and the Lorax. The author had watched the
sculptress grow; he was her step-dad, you should know. So drive
to State and Chestnut Streets to see some art that can't be beat.

Dr. Seuss and the Cat in the Hat sculpture.
Photo courtesy of Dr. Seuss properties™ & © 2004 Dr. Suess
Enterprises, L.P. (All rights reserved.) and Dr. Seuss National
Memorial Sculpture Garden, Springfield, Massachusetts. Sculptor
Lark G. Dimond-Cates lives in Southern California with her husband.
She can be reached at P.O. Box 2831, Rancho Santa Fe, CA 92067.

E L D E R   R I D E R
Springfield

Harley-Davidson was not the first major brand that came out of the motorcycle industry; that distinction belongs to the Indian Motorcycle Company, which started in Springfield. More than a motorcycle, the Indian was a way of life. The makers combined the top in technology with élan and a tradition of making great bikes. But the brand was sold in 1999, and who knows what will happen to the company. But if you want to remember the original, head to the Indian Motorcycle Museum and Hall of Fame to join the wild bunch that appreciates this part of history.

Aside from Harley-Davidson, Indian was the only one of more than two dozen American motorcycle companies that made it through the Great Depression. But Indian was on shaky ground and finally failed in the 1950s.

The museum includes the world's first Indian motorcycle, as well as a bike made of wood; aircraft engines and boat engines; the world's first snowmobile; products from other famous manufacturers; and a load of toys. There is also a replica of the first commercial motorcycle—not an Indian, but an 1885 Daimler (the original is probably still out on a road trip). To see the museum, saddle up and head to 33 Hendee Street. For more information, call (413) 737–2624. Leather jackets are optional.

EXTRA-LARGE STACK
Springfield

Most of the breakfast-going world divides into two camps: short and full stacks. Where you come down on the question is a matter of devotion and capacity because, let's face it, instead of soaring, those doughy flying saucers can pin you to the floor as efficiently as a professional wrestler. For some people, a mass of pancakes is something to avoid, while for others, it means a bigger sponge for sopping up the syrup. Do you find yourself asking, "May I have more?" If so, the answer is that you may—in May. Every May the city of Springfield hosts what it has come to call the world's largest pancake breakfast, in celebration of its anniversary. Forget any church or charity breakfast you have seen. This is the morning's first meal on a scale frightening to behold. The event takes place outside (there is no indoor venue that will do) along Main Street, from State to Bridge.

In the past few years, about 70,000 people have shown up for this feast each year, which is a huge jump from the estimated 40,000 in 1999. We are talking enough flapjacks to make a stack that is literally miles high. The Library of Congress has deemed this May-munching-madness a Local Legacy Event. Undoubtedly it happens only once a year so that the volunteers have a chance to wash all the dishes and pans in time for the next observance. If you want more information, call (413) 733–3800.

STATUESQUE
Stockbridge

W e thought that artists were supposed to be perpetually hungry and ensconced in garrets. After learning about Chesterwood, we've come to the conclusion that such stories are nothing but aggressive public relations to convince tax authorities and debt collectors to forgo phone calls and write off any owed money as unobtainable. This 122-acre estate was not even the main residence of sculptor Daniel Chester French, but rather the man's summer home and studio. Oh, well, he was in his seventies when he acquired the property, so some allowance can be made for financial endurance.

While French's name may not be immediately familiar, his work is bound to be. It includes such memorials as the seated president in the Lincoln Memorial and the Minute Man statue in Concord. There are literally dozens of his statues tucked away in

The 1920s summer home of Daniel Chester French is open from May through October.
Photo by Ron Blunt/Courtesy of Chesterwood

various parts of Massachusetts. At Chesterwood you can see models of some of French's works, as well as paintings that he's created and others that he's collected, his tools, and even exhibitions of other artists' sculpture. Enjoy the spacious Italian gardens May through October, and remember, it was a summer residence, so don't expect to wander the grounds in the off season (although there are special programs at Christmas). For more information, call (413) 298–3579, or visit www.chesterwood.org. To reach Chesterwood, go to the west end of Main Street and follow the signs to the location on Williamsville Road.

NO WICKED WITCH HERE

Tyringham

Most of us grew up with fairy tales, including the story of Hansel and Gretel, who were enticed by the gingerbread house. They had troubles, but nothing that putting a little heat on the situation couldn't cure. Those visiting Tyringham, however, can feel as cool as a cucumber while visiting the gingerbread house of Sir Henry Kitson. The edifice, which he called Santarella, was his art studio. It featured a whimsical design that made visitors feel like they were in the middle of a storybook. But whimsy can be deceptive. The studio's wavy thatched roof is actually a carefully constructed sculpture, formed from sliced dyed asphalt roof shingles set in stacks more than 1½ feet thick. Heavy chestnut beams hold the estimated eighty tons of weight.

There is a certain degree of irony that Sir Henry, a Brit, was the sculptor of the Puritan Maid in Plymouth. He was also responsible for the Minute Man statue in Lexington, commemorating a war in which, to put it nicely, our side whooped his.

(The statue is not to be confused with the Minute Man in Concord, created by Daniel Chester French, whose former house is now a museum in Stockbridge.) Some of Kitson's other works include statues of Robert E. Lee and Jefferson Davis, so his subjects weren't always on the winning side.

Like French, Kitson built his getaway when he hit his seventies. Perhaps on a small scale, Kitson struck one for Britain, taking the money he made in statues of the political elite and in memorials and hiring workers from the United Kingdom to build his roof. But he was reputedly an incredibly difficult man to work for, so we wonder how many came to wish that the project's roof would just cave in.

Santarella is open from Memorial Day through the end of October and is at 75 Main Road. Not only can you visit the museum and gardens, but there are even overnight guest rooms to rent here—just make sure you have easy access to the oven. Call (413) 243–3260 for more information.

THE BIG SQUEEZE
Washington

If you have a taste for French cafes, Cajun two-stepping, Italian weddings, or just a lively polka band, we have an event for you. Something that all four have in common is the accordion—or squeeze box, to use the more down-home and eclectic title. The instrument has been the butt of humor for years, whether called a concertina or a button box. Yet to its devotees, there is nothing more endearing than the reedy, wheezy sound produced by this family of miniature, portable, wind-driven pianos. In Amherst there is a shop that specializes in the sales and repairs of accordions and concertinas. Obviously the management has a soft spot in their hearts (and, those who don't like the sound would say, in their heads) for the instruments and those who love them.

And so, to promote camaraderie (and presumably sales) the store, called the Button Box, began to organize and sponsor the Northeast Squeeze-In Festival in Washington. Every September it sports what is undoubtedly the largest collection of players who gather to do nothing but to press their own buttons, if not each other's. The gathering takes place at Bucksteep Manor, an estate on Washington Mountain Road. For more information, call (413) 549–0171 or visit www.buttonbox.com.

FORWARD INTO THE PAST
West Springfield

Have your kids seen any of the television programs in which modern families live in the setting of some earlier era—whether Edwardian, frontier time, or Pilgrim? They can actually have a taste of it themselves at Storrowton Village, a re-creation of a nineteenth-century New England community, complete with town green. Kids can spend a day or even a week dressed in period clothing, trying their hand at such crafts as candle dipping and tile mosaics, milking a cow, and spinning wool and weaving. If they are going for the day, the kids bring their own lunch. (What, there was a time without Big Macs?) For longer visits, meals are provided.

We bet that no matter how good the program, your children won't return ready to haul the water or feed the pigs. But at least you'll have a few days of relative quiet. For more information, call (413) 205–5051, or visit www.thebige.com/ storrowton.html to check programs and events.

A NOSE FOR BUSINESS
West Stockbridge

When things go well, most businesspeople would not say that they smell. But a heavy aroma is a good sign at Charles H. Baldwin and Sons, a shop established in 1888 and dedicated to the proposition that not all vanillas are created equal. The store is a major source of upscale vanilla extract—a distillation of the fruit of tropical orchids. And here the dismissive phrase "plain vanilla" is a euphemism for "unbelievably expensive." Baldwin's uses only Madagascar Bourbon vanilla beans distilled in a copper apparatus that is over sixty-five years old. They then age it in hundred-year-old oak barrels to add to the flavoring and color. When Charles Baldwin started his business, he went by horse and buggy from door to door. Today orders come in from chefs and demanding amateur cooks from around the world over the Web site (www.baldwinextracts.com). But as good as vanilla is, the current owners, the Moffatt family, have branched out to such flavors as lemon, almond, and peppermint. They also have a Worcestershire sauce and a maple syrup with walnuts and (what else?) vanilla, both from old recipes the Moffatts found in the store.

Years ago many women used a dab of vanilla instead of perfume. Men who might feel a bit uncomfortable doing the same can pick up a bottle of Baldwin's bay rum. Accept no substitutes, as you'll "nose" the difference. The shop is at 1 Center Street, (413) 232–7785.

INDEX

ABOUT THE AUTHORS

Bruce Gellerman is an international award-winning journalist with more than twenty years' experience in radio, print, and television, including creating and hosting the popular public radio show *Here & Now*. Journalist **Erik Sherman**'s writing and photographs have appeared in many national publications, and he is the author of *Geocaching: Hike and Seek with Your GPS*.